INCREDIBLE FOOTBALL FEATS

brings you astonishing events from all aspects of the game—from high-school ball, the colleges, and the pros!

Here are the answers to such questions as: What player scored 395 points in one season? • Who holds all-time scoring records for *three* pro football teams? • What quarterback rushed 38 times during one pro game? • What 5'9", 161-pound player rushed for 350 yards in one Big Ten game? • Who set an NFL field-goal record on his first try as a pro? • Has a woman ever played pro football? • Who were the seven brothers who once played for the same pro football team? • What rush for 98 yards failed to score?

And many more incredible feats of scoring, rushing, passing and receiving, kicking, defense, coaching, and team records!

Incredible Football Feats

By Jim Benagh

tempo books

GROSSET & DUNLAP
Publishers   New York

Portions of the Korshalla Feat beginning on p. 3 have been
adapted from "The Record-Breaking Ringer" which appeared
in *True* Magazine, copyright 1973 by Fawcett Publications.

Photo Credits:
p. 1, Ken Hall; pp. 2, 5, 8, 9 (top), 12-13 (bottom), 15 (bottom), U.P.I.; p. 3 (bottom), N.A.I.A.; p. 3 (top), Widener
College; pp. 4, 16 (top), Pro Football Hall of Fame; pp. 6
(top), 10 (top), 11, Wide World Photos; p. 6 (bottom),
Michigan State University; p. 7, North Park College; p. 9
(bottom), New York Jets; p. 10 (bottom), Houston Oilers;
p. 12 (top), University of Alabama; p. 13 (top), University of
Michigan; p. 14, *Orlando SENTINEL STAR;* p. 15 (top),
Tony Capozzoli; p. 16 (bottom), Dallas Cowboys.

For my mother

Contents

PASSING AND RECEIVING

KICKING

DEFENSE

COACHING

TEAM RECORDS

MISCELLANEOUS

Foreword

Sports feats have held my fascination for years, ever since I grew up in Northern Michigan. While in high school at Cheboygan, Michigan, we had a fabulous fullback who set a state record with 153 points and scored nearly 350 points in his prep career. But I learned then that the circumstances of such feats can be as interesting as the records themselves. Our scoring star, Tommy McGinn, averaged about 30 yards on his scoring jaunts, but the touchdown that gave Tommy the record was only two inches. As for his total points, which may have constituted another record, several of them were tallied in his freshman year at another local high school, where he played six-man football.

The unusual feats are where you find 'em, whether it's in Cheboygan, Michigan, or the New York Public Library, or the dusty archives of the Wheeling (West Virginia) Library, where a person can get the black lung disease searching through old newspapers in that coal-mining center. I know; that's where I dug out the information about Joe Korshalla (see page 7). Letters and telephone calls to the people who accomplished the feats corrected some misconceptions, too.

Some of the greatest—or at least most interesting—football feats in this book aren't "records" at all in the official sense. For instance, there is no official clearing house for high-school records, as there is in pro and college football. However, with diligent research one can find that the high-school player who caught 23 passes in one game played another game in which he got 13 in the final quarter when his team was behind.

Bert Rechichar's National Football League record for longest field goal has since been surpassed after 17 years on the books, but the way that he accomplished his feat is still unmatched for intrigue. My old friend and mentor Bennie Oosterbaan set many records as a player, but his feat of coaching a national championship team at the University of Michigan on his first try stands out more in my mind. Those are the incredible football feats that I have searched for to include in this book.

I've discarded some of the so-called "official records" for their cheapness, such as John Reaves' passing record at the University of Florida. In Florida's last game with Miami, the one in which Reaves needed to accumulate some yardage to get his record, his own team gave up a touchdown on defense in order to get the ball back on offense for its star quarterback. That strategy wasn't even unique; the University of Washington had done the same thing back in the early 1950s for Don Heinrich.

But I'll let the reader be the final judge as to what constitutes *Incredible Football Feats*.

Acknowledging all of the people who have helped me gather football facts over the years would be impossible. Some of the persons who helped me most with this book, however, were Jerry Klein and others at the National Collegiate Athletic Bureau; Herman Masin, *Scholastic Magazines;* Jim Bukata and other public relations staffers of the National Association of Intercollegiate Athletics (NAIA); the National Football League staff, particularly Don Weiss, Harold Rosenthal and Jim Heffernan; Jim Campbell of the Pro Football Hall of Fame; and Doug Huff, sports department of the Wheeling (West Virginia) *Intelligencer,* who has become a one-man clearing house for high-school sports records. Many players, coaches, college sports information directors and newspapermen have generously contributed their time and ideas. To all of them go my thanks.

As a final note, the author would appreciate hearing from football record buffs in the future— for possible additions to *Incredible Football*

Feats. Please write c/o Post Office Box 1113, Englewood Cliffs, N. J. 07632.

Jim Benagh
May, 1974

SCORING

Korshalla Scored 71 Points In A College Game—But Was He A Collegian?

The Sunday sports pages of November 20, 1932, were about as bleak as the fog and snow that blanketed the playing fields of the nation's colleges the day before. Yale beat Harvard in "The Game" by a whopping but dull 19-0 score, the largest margin in three decades between the teams. Old Man Stagg closed out his 41-year career at the University of Chicago with a disappointing loss to Wisconsin. Even the pros were uninteresting. The old New York *Herald-Tribune* had advanced the feature NFL battle between the New York Giants and the Green Bay Packers as "the most attractive game on the home list," but saw fit to give the contest only three paragraphs on page eight.

If there was any bright football news that dull day, it had to be the report out of Wheeling, West Virginia, where a small-college freshman made football history. His name was Joe Korshalla. The papers heralded his feats on their front sports pages—and spelled his name "Kershalla."

Joe Korshalla was a bowling-ball type of halfback of Polish–Slavic descent from the coal-mining country near Wilkes-Barre, Pennsylvania, who wound up on the campus of West Liberty Normal a few years after he got out of high school. Balding "Cueball" Korshalla had been a big name in high school, but his contributions to the West Virginia teachers college in 1932 were minimal—until November 19. He had scored only one touchdown from his post at halfback. The fuzzy newspaper reports of that season say he was often injured.

But West Liberty's final opponent of the year, Cedarville College, was ripe for a bright performance by Korshalla and the other West Liberty "Hilltoppers." Cedarville's "Yellowjackets" had been outscored, 268-7, in their previous seven losses.

Korshalla was the first Hilltopper to take advantage of Cedarville's discouraged legions. The first time he got the ball, in the opening minute of play, he rambled 70 yards for a touchdown. It set the tone for the West Liberty team. *Every time* the Hilltoppers got the ball in the first half, they scored. As the half neared its completion, and Cedarville neared its depletion, it was decided to cut down the playing time. The first half would

8

be only 24 minutes instead of the normal 30; the second half would be made up of two ten-minute quarters.

Even then, West Liberty had an 83-0 halftime lead and Korshalla had racked up six TDs, all of them over 22 yards.

In the second half, West Liberty got more benevolent and pulled out all of the first-stringers except Korshalla. But that didn't stop Korshalla from going for the collegiate record for TDs, points and yards rushing in a single game.

He made four more TDs going into the final minute of the shortened game. Also along the way, he kicked five extra points. Then in the waning seconds, he got off a 75-yard punt return for his eleventh TD. But it was called back because of a clip by a teammate who was playing his first game. West Liberty held Cedarville, though, and got the ball back. Korshalla ran from scrimmage one last time and went 35 yards for a TD that counted.

The game ended but the statisticians didn't.

It took over three hours to sort through the maze of figures and find out just exactly what West Liberty and Korshalla had done—besides winning, 137-0. The official tallies gave Korshalla 11 TDs, none of them less than 22 yards and most of them over 40; 5 extra points; and 504 yards rushing in 20 carries. The 71 points remains a collegiate record, having eclipsed the 68 points scored—by a *West Liberty player*—the year before.

Korshalla disappeared from the college football scene almost as fast as he arrived on it. The school—now West Liberty State College—admits that he may not have been a student after all; the official historian can find no proof that he ever enrolled. "It might be that he was a ringer," said Art Barbeau, who claims to be the "official drum beater" for West Liberty sports. When asked if Korshalla had any teammates who could solve the mystery, Barbeau replied, "Try a guy over in Follansbee who played for West Liberty for eight straight years."

Korshalla's widow was tracked down in Pennsylvania, and even she was at a loss to explain why her husband, who died several years ago, used two different spellings for his last name. "He didn't talk much about football," she said.

The next year, 1933, a new football coach was in and scholarships were out—a Depression kid could no longer trade his talent on a football field for room and board at West Liberty. But Joe Korshalla left another mark before he packed his bags and returned to the coal country. In the spring of 1933, West Liberty Normal met Rio Grande College in a baseball doubleheader. The next day, the Sunday papers were reporting how a Joe *Kershalla*, batting cleanup, smacked four triples for what may be another record of some sort.

To this day, Korshalla's record 71 points is in the NCAA's official football record book. Appropriately, they spell the mysterious man's name *Kershalla.*

Hall Scored 395 Points In A Season, 899 In His High-School Career

Kenneth Hall of Sugar Land (Texas) High School could do just about anything he wanted to as a high-school football star. Consider, for example, his greatest game for the small-town team on the outskirts of Houston, Texas. It was 1953, Hall's senior year, and he was setting records that no prep has come close to matching. Hall was aiming for the state one-game scoring record set by a player named Dick Todd, who himself had tallied 318 points one season and 664 in his career at Crowell High. Todd had scored 48 points in one game.

Hall had matched that 48 points with time to play against Houston Lutheran. En route to that total, he had rushed for 520 yards in only 11 attempts for an average of 47.3 a try and returned a kickoff 64 yards and a punt 82 yards for TDs. As Sugar Land's place-kicker, Hall knew that

Todd's single-game mark was within his reach. But as Sugar Land lined up for the extra point, Hall, unbeknown to his teammates, took off running with the ball instead of kicking it. A 205-pounder with 9.7 speed in the 100-yard dash, he made it as usual.

The 49 points was miniscule compared to Hall's other records. As a senior, he scored 395 points in 12 games, two of which were state play-off contests. In his career, he scored 899. Of the latter, 841 points were racked up in his final three years.

Hall rushed for 4045 yards—about 337 yards a game—as a senior. He accumulated 11,232 in his prep career. Considering that recent unofficial prep records list Joe Wylie's 6730 as the "best" career mark, Hall's forgotten heroics are astonishing.

Surprisingly, Kenneth Hall's career got a belated start at Sugar Land. He didn't go out for football right away in his freshman year. But after the team lost its first three games, the school principal assembled the boys among the 130 Sugar Land students and asked for their support. Hall and several other freshmen and sophomores answered the call. Sugar Land lost only one game in four years after that—and that was the one in which Hall did not play.

As a football newcomer, Hall mostly passed. But later he was installed as a tailback for Coach L. V. Hightower's teams, taking the snap from

13

center in the Notre Dame box formation about 5 yards behind the line of scrimmage. There was no stopping him.

Hightower still recalls the game against Orchard High in which Hall called for a "box right" play in which he would carry the ball. Hall went 80 yards for the TD. But the officials called it back because of a penalty. Hall called for a "box left" and went 85 yards on the next play.

It was after that second play that officials called for a time out. Hightower, wondering why the ensuing kickoff was held up, summoned the officials for an explanation. No problem, they said, they were just tired out!

After completing his high-school career, Hall went to Texas A&M. His bubble burst in a conflict of philosophy with Head Coach Paul (Bear) Bryant. Hall did not get to play much as a sophomore and dropped out of school. In 1956, he joined the Edmonton Eskimos of the Canadian League and was a starter for their Grey Cup championship team.

A few years later he returned to the Houston area to play for the Oiler team of the new American Football League. As an AFL rookie, he got back into the record books again—this time with a 104-yard kickoff return. It's still an all-time best for that team.

Ken Hall's Record

As a freshman in 1950, Ken Hall scored 58 points in 7 games. In 1951, 224 points in 12 games. In 1952, 222 points in 11 games. And finally in 1953, his record season, 395 points in 12 games. Below is a table of that incredible 1953 season.

S.L.	Sugar Land Scores	Opp.	Hall's Scores TDs	P.A.T.	Total Pts.
40	Katy	14	4	4	28
53	Missouri City	18	6	5	41
45	Needville	7	3	3	21
73	Houston Lutheran	14	7	7	49
41	Van Vleck	7	5	5	35
41	Klein	18	5	5	35
67	Orchard	19	5	7	37
59	Danbury	12	7	5	47
47	Pearland	13	4	5	29
46	Barber's Hill	12	6	3	39
	Playoff Games				
33	Chester	13	3	3	21
13	Magnolia	6	2	1	13

Blanda Holds All-Time Scoring Records For 3 Pro Football Teams

As ageless George Blanda approached his 25th professional football season in 1974, he spoke about the art of place-kicking. "It's conceivable that I could kick forever," he said. "Physically, playing golf is tougher."

It seems that George Blanda has indeed been playing forever. The second game of the 1973 season was his 300th as a professional. His 24 seasons were far and away more than any other player recorded. Runnerup Johnny Unitas, in fact, has introduced George at banquets as "my boyhood hero." Blanda has played almost 100 more games than Unitas and nearly 200 in a row.

Place-kicking, of course, is what has kept Blanda active for so long. He's been somewhat of a "relief pitcher" as a quarterback while in his forties, a feat that helped earn him Player of the Year honors as late as 1970. But as far as moving the ball is concerned, he hasn't scored a touchdown since 1960.

Kicking the ball has been a Blanda specialty since he came into pro football with the Chicago Bears in 1949. His records are so numerous that they would need pages to tell. But his greatest feat may be that of holding the all-time scoring records for three of pro football's 26 teams.

Blanda left the Chicago Bears in 1958. But he took the Bear record of 541 points with him. No one has been able to get that back despite the expanded schedules and added emphasis on field goals since that time.

Blanda sat out the 1959 season. People thought he was over the hill at age 32. But he came back with the new Houston Oiler team of the American Football League in 1960. He came close to leading the AFL in scoring that first campaign with 115 points. Before the Oilers gave up on him in 1966, he established a team record of 598 points that still stands.

The Oakland Raiders were quick to pick up Blanda as a back up quarterback and placekicker. He did not disappoint them in either category, becoming famous for his last-minute heroics as a clutch passer and kicker. At one stretch, he made 201 conversions in a row and had another skein of 105 going into 1974. He scored a team-record 703 points in seven seasons as a Raider.

Altogether, Blanda has scored 1842 points as a pro. Along with nine touchdowns, he has made

855 of 865 points-after-touchdowns and 311 of 610 field goals. Nine of his field goals have traveled 50 yards or more.

All-time runnerup Lou Groza (retired) had 1349 points.

How great are his records?

A place-kicker in these days of the specialist is considered to have a fine season if he scores 100 points in a year, as Blanda did in 1973. A newcomer in the league would thus need about 18 fine seasons to catch up with him.

Then again, a newcomer might just be chasing smoke. Blanda said after the 1973 season that he had no plans to retire, partly because he had no other career to pursue. "I'm too old to coach," he joked.

George Blanda's Record

Team	Year	TD	P.A.T.	FG	Total
Chicago	1949	1	0	7-15	27
"	1950	0	0	6-15	18
"	1951	0	26-26	6-17	44
"	1952	1	30-30	6-25	54
"	1953	0	27-27	7-20	48
"	1954	0	23-23	8-16	47
"	1955	2	37-37	11-16	82
"	1956	0	45-47	12-28	81
"	1957	1	23-23	14-26	71
"	1958	0	36-37	11-23	69
	1959		Did not play		

Scoring

Houston	1960	4	46-47	15-34	115
"	1961	0	64-65	16-26	112
"	1962	0	48-49	11-26	81
"	1963	0	39-39	9-22	66
"	1964	0	37-38	13-29	76
"	1965	0	28-28	11-21	61
"	1966	0	39-40	16-30	87
Oakland	1967	0	56-57	20-30	116
"	1968	0	54-54	21-34	117
"	1969	0	45-45	20-37	105
"	1970	0	36-36	16-29	84
"	1971	0	41-42	15-22	86
"	1972	0	44-44	17-26	95
"	1973	0	31-31	23-33	100

Montgomery Scored 37 Touchdowns During His Freshman Year In College

Wilbert Montgomery wasn't exactly what you would call a highly sought-after prospect during his senior year of high school in 1972. The reason was fairly simple: he played defensive back most of the time while his younger brother Cleotha handled the rushing chores at their Greenville, Mississippi, high school.

Montgomery found the end zone in college, however, after Abilene Christian College in Texas gave him a scholarship. In fact, he found it a record 37 times in 1973. Not since 1926, when a player named Mayes McLain of Haskell Institute had scored 38 times, had a player found the goal line so often in one season. But in 1926 collegiate records were unofficial.

The Abilene road-runner scored 31 of his TDs in regular-season play and led the team into the NAIA post-season tournament. He needed only nine games to top the modern college record in regular season play (29, by Lydell Mitchell, Penn State). Then, in the playoffs, he scored four times in a semifinal victory over Langston (Oklahoma) University and two more times against Elon (North Carolina) College as his team easily won the NAIA title. His 224 total points was another modern record.

For his first year, he rushed for 1181 yards and averaged 6.5 yards a carry.

As a final bonus to the school that took a chance on him in 1973, Montgomery announced that his brother would follow him to the school, possibly as a defensive back.

* * *

During his freshman season, the 5' 11", 190-pound Montgomery got in on a record performance which only indirectly was of his making.

Abilene Christian had lost its opening game, 56-46, and almost matched the all-time record for most points by a losing team—49. Two games later, Montgomery raced into the end zone in the final minute of a game against Stephen F. Austin University for his sixth touchdown of the day. The final score: Abilene Christian 57, S. F. Austin 50!

Johnson Set A College Record
For Long-Distance Touchdowns

Billy Johnson was a 9.5 sprinter on the track team for little Widener College of Chester, Pennsylvania, in the 1970s. But by college football measuring sticks, he was a long-distance star.

A native of Marcus Hook, Pennsylvania, Johnson chose the college near his home because he wanted a nearby school where his father could see him play. He had to sit out his first season—1971—because of an eligibility problem, but he worked his way into the starting lineup as a sophomore in 1972. He sparkled right from the start. Carrying the ball about 10 times a game, he gained over 100 yards rushing for three straight weeks. He also scored two touchdowns in each of the games.

Coach Bill Manlove of Widener began wondering about the phenomenal prospect he had in the fold and a decision was made to move the

5′ 8½″, 170-pounder from slotback to running back. "We just weren't feeding him the ball enough," said Manlove. "But then we began wondering if he would be tough enough in the new position because he had difficulty gaining 100 yards there in a game. The week later we stopped wondering—he gained 200 yards."

As a slotback, Johnson had scored three TDs—averaging 32.3 yards for his jaunts. As a running back, he began ripping off touchdown runs of unbelievable lengths.

In three years on the varsity, Johnson would run from scrimmage for 51 touchdowns. The average length of his scoring bursts on rushes was 35.9 yards. As a punt returner, he dashed for seven more touchdowns, averaging 81.2 yards for each breakaway. He also returned one kickoff for 85 yards.

Altogether Billy Johnson scored 62 touchdowns in his career, and the average length of those twisting, sprinting tallies was 41.7 yards—far and away an NCAA record. He also had seven other TDs called back because of penalties. Their average length: 60.0 yards.

As a ball-handler, Johnson scored a touchdown each 7.7 times he rushed, caught a pass, or returned a kick. It broke the mark set by West Point's Doc Blanchard (one TD per 8.2 attempts), who starred during the World War II years when Army had a monopoly on the best college players. Johnson also wiped out the record of 246.3 "all-purpose yards" set by another Hall of Fame star, Colorado's Whizzer White. Billy had 251.6 yards on rushes, receptions and returns each game in one season.

All in all, Johnson set nine NCAA records. Besides the TD Frequency and All-Purpose marks, he got his name in the archives for:

Rushing, career yards per carry
   (min.: 300) 9.1
Rushing, season yards per carry
   (min.: 140) 10.5
Scoring, points per game, career 13.2
Touchdowns per game, career 2.2
Total points, three seasons 372
Total touchdowns, three seasons 62
Average touchdown distance
   (min.: 35 TDs) 41.7

* * *

If Johnson's feats were well chronicled, there was a reason. Before Billy came along, Coach Manlove had had another running back who threatened the record book. Richie Weaver had rushed for 363 yards in a game, but was taken out with six minutes to play because the score was out of hand. Later Manlove learned that Weaver's performance had been just 10 yards short of the NCAA record for rushing yards in a game.

"We vowed after that that we were going to keep a record book in the press box," said the coach.

After Johnson completed his three years at Widener, the school had to get another record book—the one that the elusive halfback had rewritten.

Byrge Scored 78 Points In A High-School Game When They Weren't Enough

Eddie Byrge of Huntsville (Tennessee) High School went into the final game of the 1968 season needing 81 points to overtake the state scoring leader. Byrge had already tallied 150 for the year.

But 81 points?

Some players would be happy to score that many for a whole season.

Byrge gave it a try, though. Rushing for 424 yards against Sunbright High, he began finding the end zone time and time again. And each time he scored, he would try for the conversion, too. By the end of the day, he had a total of 78 points as his team scored an even 100. Nobody said whether he was disappointed or not. His one-game figure is an unofficial national record.

* * *

Ernie Perea of Los Lunas, New Mexico, put together the previous unofficial record. It happened the year before, in 1967.

Perea trampled Fort Wingate High all day long as he scored a total of 77 points.

His team won, 78-6.

The history books don't say what happened to the other point, the one that would have kept him up with Byrge.

* * *

Among 70-point-plus scorers, Don Gullet of South Shore, Kentucky's McKell High School had the perfect game on November 8, 1968: He scored all 72 of his team's points in a 72-7 thrashing of Wurtland High School. He made 11 touchdowns and six of the conversions. En route to the goal line, he rushed for 430 yards. His touchdowns ranged from 3 to 95 yards.

There was a reason behind Gullet's splurge, according to the star player. "Our coach was mad at the other coach," he said.

Gullet also scored 47 points in a single basketball game and pitched a few no-hitters in baseball. While he was still a teenager, he made it to the big leagues with the Cincinnati Reds.

As for his old high school, they dropped football not too long after he graduated. Maybe it was because he won too many game balls.

RUSHING

Feathers Set A Record For Yards Per Rush That Has Stood For 4 Decades

Beattie Feathers was as light-footed a runner as his last name suggests. He entered the National Football League in 1934, just two seasons after the league began keeping statistical records, and he put together a portfolio that the pros are still using as a yardstick in comparing the great runners. The 25-year-old rookie, fresh out of the University of Tennessee, is credited with a 9.94-yards-per-carry average that season. No one has come within 3 yards per carry of that mark.

The 5′ 11″, 188-pound speedster was groomed to be Red Grange's replacement with the Chicago Bears that season. After a couple of games, Grange himself became Feathers' greatest booster.

In his first game, against the Green Bay Packers, Feathers made a credible showing, as he gained 41 yards in eight carries. But after that opener, his performances were incredible. Week after week, Feathers was ripping off yardage at almost 10 yards a try. He gained 140 in his second outing at Cincinnati, 132 at Brooklyn, 101 at Pittsburgh and so on.

After 11 games, Feathers' ledger showed 1004 yards, something no pro before him had done and no other pro would do until 1947. Then he got injured and missed the last two games of the Bears' unbeaten season.

The National Football League, in tallying up Feathers' yardage, charged him with 101 attempts from scrimmage, thus giving him his 9.94-yard average. However, Jim Campbell, of the Pro Football Hall of Fame at Canton, Ohio, has since reported that his research in sketchy game stories indicates that Feathers lugged the ball 117 times, which would give him an 8.58 mean. Whatever the figure, it's still well above the runnerup average of 6.87 yards set in 1972 by Bear quarterback Bobby Douglass.

Feathers, a popular man who later coached at Wake Forest, always cited good blocking for his 1934 feat. "I played behind the greatest blocker ever, Bronko Nagurski," he told banquet audiences who asked about his stellar performance.

Strangely enough, Feathers never gained a total of 1000 yards in all the pro games he played in the next six years. And his per-carry average was never more than 5.0 a try. But for one season, he was as good as one could be.

Feathers' Game-By-Game Statistics
In His Record 1934 Season

	Attempts*	Yards	Longest Run
at Green Bay	8	41	19
at Cincinnati	18	140	32
at Brooklyn	14	132	29
at Pittsburgh	8	101	82
at Chicago Cards	15	97	27
Cincinnati	7	114	34
Green Bay	15	155	31
New York Giants	8	55	21
at Boston	11	80	24
at N.Y. Giants	10	47	12
Chicago Cards	3	42	20
at Detroit	(injured)		
Detroit	(injured)		
Totals	117*	1004	82

(*According to the Pro Football Hall of Fame; NFL credits
Feathers with 101 attempts.)

Simpson Topped 2000 Yards Rushing To Smash The NFL Mark

As a teenager, O. J. Simpson once met Jimmy Brown, the famous No. 32 of the Cleveland Browns, when the pro football star was visiting Simpson's neighborhood in San Francisco. "You ain't so tough," O. J. told him. "I'll break your record some day."

It was a brash statement; Jimmy Brown was universally regarded as the best running back in the game at the time—if not the best in pro football history. When Jimmy Brown set records, they were supposed to stay put. For eight of his nine years as a pro, Brown led the NFL in rushing, and he might have extended that accomplishment if he had not retired while he was at his peak. Of all of Brown's records, though, the single-season total of 1863 yards in the rushing department seemed the most invincible.

Jimmy Brown also had the second best rushing

mark for a season (1544 yards) and the third best (1527).

But then came O. J., sporting the same No. 32 that Brown made famous.

The resemblance ended with the number. O. J., with his 9.3-second speed in the 100-yard dash, was more of a Gale Sayers type, only bigger. Brown was bullish although he too had good speed. Brown was more of a fullback, Simpson a halfback.

Simpson's fancy stepping style was misleading, according to the man who did the stepping. "I may not always look it," he said in 1973, "But I'm aggressive. You have to be to be a good football player, or a good anything."

In 1973 Simpson was as good a football player as ever lived. After years on the brink of real stardom with the downtrodden Buffalo Bills, Simpson was given a supporting cast of blockers who could fortify his breakaway talents. The Bills had been drafting top collegians for years to bolster their offensive line.

Simpson made good use of his help.

Beginning with a record 250-yard outburst in his opening game against the New England Patriots, Simpson startled the football world. And some opposing coaches: "It was like a track meet out there," said the Patriots' Chuck Fairbanks. "O. J. looked like Grant going through Richmond."

O. J.'s 200-yard-plus game was only the 20th

in football history. But after continuing the season at an unbelievable pace, Simpson finished with two more 200-yard days. In the end, the new No. 32 made Brown's records look merely mortal.

Simpson's Records in 1973

Yards rushing, one game—250, vs. New England; previous record, 247, by Willie Ellison, Los Angeles, 1971.

Yards rushing, one season—2003; previous record, 1863, by Jimmy Brown, 1963.

Most games of 100 or more yards, one season—10; previous record, 9, by Jimmy Brown, 1963.

Most attempts rushing, one game—39, vs. Kansas City; previous record, 38, by Harry Newman, New York Giants, 1934, and Jim Nance, Boston, 1966.

Most attempts rushing, one season—332; previous record, 305, by Jimmy Brown, Cleveland, 1963.

Game-by-Game Rushing

O. J. SIMPSON			JIM BROWN		
	Carries	Yds.		Carries	Yds.
New England	29	250	Washington	15	162
San Diego	22	103	Dallas	20	232
N.Y. Jets	24	123	Los Angeles	22	95
Philadelphia	27	171	Pittsburgh	21	175
Baltimore	22	166	N.Y. Giants	23	123
Miami	14	55	Philadelphia	25	144
Kansas City	39	157	N.Y. Giants	9	40
New Orleans	20	79	Philadelphia	28	223
Cincinnati	20	99	Pittsburgh	19	99
Miami	20	120	St. Louis	22	154
Baltimore	15	124	Dallas	17	51
Atlanta	24	137	St. Louis	29	179
New England	22	219	Detroit	13	61
N.Y. Jets	34	200	Washington	28	125
Total	332	2003	Total	291	1863

Newman, A Quarterback, Rushed 38 Times During A Pro Football Game

With recent vintage rushers like Jimmy Brown and O. J. Simpson on the scene, no ball-carrying records could be regarded as sacred. Their names saturate the all-time lists. But there were 60 minutes back in 1934 when a quarterback had his fun carrying the ball, too.

On November 11 of that year, Harry Newman's New York Giant team was locked in a tight battle with the Green Bay Packers before an Armistice Day crowd of 27,000. The score was 3-3 at the half, and Packer coach Curley Lambeau was living up to his pre-game boast that his team would give the championship-bound Giants "plenty of exercise."

The person who got the biggest workout was Newman.

In the first half, Newman took a lateral from halfback Ken Strong, who started the play on his own 5, and zigzagged most of the way downfield before ferrying the ball to another Giant, Red Badgro, who carried the ball into the end zone. However, officials ruled that Newman had stepped out of bounds.

In the second half, Newman began taking matters into his own hands. Injuries and other problems were plaguing his backfield mates, so he began carrying the ball himself.

After playing like an iron man as he rushed over and over, Newman cut inside left tackle for a 12-yard gain, then bulled past five Packers to get into the end zone. Newman carried for 50 of the Giants' 58 yards on that drive.

Later in the third period, Newman was at it again, thrusting forward 11 yards to the Packer 3-yard line after a fumble. From there, Newman plowed into the end zone again.

In the final period, Newman helped his teammates eat up the clock and maintain field position with more and more quarterback runs. He also found enough energy to dodge past three Packers and nail Clark Hinkle for a touchdown-saving tackle.

When they added up the statistics for that game, which the Giants won, 17-3, Newman was credited with a record 38 carries. Though his total yardage was only 117, he had established a mark for rushing attempts that would remain for almost four decades. It took O. J. Simpson to break it in 1973.

Allen Of Michigan State University Gained 350 Yards Rushing In A Game

When they nicknamed Eric Allen "The Flea" his friends knew what they were doing. Not only was he buggish-sized (a 5′ 9″, 161-pounder) for a football player, but he was a real pest in the eyes of his Big Ten opponents.

Despite his lack of size, "The Flea" was a durable back who set numerous rushing records at Michigan State by the time he finished there in 1971. He set marks for most carries in a career and most yards in a game, season and career. The records are even more impressive when one realizes that he played flanker for part of his career.

As a senior in 1971, however, Allen was all running back.

He proved that on October 30 on the natural grass at Purdue University's Ross-Ade Stadium. Purdue was usually a thorn in Michigan State's side, and 1971 was expected to bring more of the same. But Coach Duffy Daugherty had modified his wishbone formation to make use of Allen's rare talent.

"What we are doing is setting up a foot race to the sidelines," said Duffy. "If we win it, and get by their contain, then a play can go for a long gainer. The great thing is that it gives a good' running back like Allen a chance to utilize his skills."

Allen found the sidelines that Saturday. And the end zone, too. Before the day was over, he had scored on runs of 24, 59, 30 and 25 yards to lead Michigan State to a 43-10 victory.

Before that final 25-yard jaunt, however, the word got out that the Georgetown, S. C., native needed only 22 yards to set the NCAA record. Daugherty got the message from the press box. The game was well in hand by then, but Duffy pulled his star tailback aside and told him, "I'm sending you back in and will give you the ball every time until you get it."

Allen failed to gain a yard on his first attempt after returning to the field; then he went all the way for a TD on his next try. His 25 yards topped the record of 347 set by Michigan's Ron Johnson (vs. Wisconsin, 1968) by 3.

Allen needed 29 carries to establish his record.

"Man, I like that natural grass," he later said.

In addition to his rushes, "The Flea" caught two passes for 47 more yards. Altogether that gave him 397 yards, and reminded sportswriters of another lithe back who had romped over the Big Ten football playing fields 47 years before. On another October day, Red Grange had gained 402 yards with his runs, passes and kick returns —and that was considered the greatest Big Ten performance ever. Allen wasn't greedy. Being close to Red Grange's performance was a pretty good credential.

PASSING
AND RECEIVING

North Park College's QB Threw 10 TD Passes In A Game—And Its Favorite Receiver Scored 8 Times

October 12, 1968 was homecoming for little North Park College in Chicago, and the theme was "Success in '68." Since 1968 was in its final quarter there wasn't too much time left to achieve the success, so quarterback Bruce Swanson took matters into his own hands.

Swanson, who happened to be engaged to the homecoming queen, got the game with North Central College off to a rousing start by spiraling a 59-yard touchdown pass to end Paul Zaeske on the first play of the game from scrimmage. The crowd of about 3,000 partisans at North Park Athletic Field was in ecstasy. But that was only the beginning.

The collegiate record for touchdown passes in a game (a *whole* game) was eight. Swanson threw for that many in the first half alone. The fact that North Park was overwhelming its downtrodden opponent by halftime, having scored on ten of its 20 offensive plays, meant that Swanson would be limited in playing time for the second half. As it turned out, he got into the game for only five more plays. But he made the best of it, throwing for two more TDs to boost his all-time single-game college record to ten.

In order, Swanson's scoring passes were for distances of 59, 5, 31, 20, 6, 32, 6, 10, 34 and 6 yards. In all, he completed 20 of 29 passes for 345 yards.

A feat even more incredible than Swanson's TD pitches was the eight TD catches made by Paul Zaeske, who later played in the National Football League. One of those scoring receptions came from Swanson's substitute.

The final score of the game was 104-32, giving North Park another NCAA college-division record for points in a game.

In all, North Park set 18 school records that day, thanks mostly to the quick hand of Swanson. But he was no newcomer to the record book. The year before he was quick-footed, too, setting an NCAA small-college record with his 46.3-yard punting average.

Haden-To-McKay Meant Sure Scoring Strikes For Bishop Amat High In California

If there was one trend that stood out in high-school football at the advent of the 1970s, it was the emergence of great passing combinations. As the Sesame Street crowd began tuning into those pro football games on television, youngsters picked up tips from the pro combos and began emulating them. In no time at all, preps from Connecticut to California began putting together statistics that would make the pros look on in awe.

The finest prep combination of all, however, lived in the home of Southern Cal football coach John McKay. One was his son J. K., a receiver, and the other was J. K.'s neighborhood buddy Pat Haden. Both attended Bishop Amat High School in the Los Angeles suburbs. As a senior,

Haden moved in with the McKays so that he could continue his career at that school.

During the period 1968–70, Haden threw 850 passes and completed 527. McKay caught 207 of them. In all, Haden threw for 82 touchdowns and McKay scored 48 times. Haden's 7633 passing yardage for three years is an unofficial all-time high-school record. In his senior year alone, he hurled 377 passes and completed 224 for 3273 yards and 42 touchdowns.

McKay reached his statistical peak as a junior when he caught a total of 106 passes for an unofficial national record. He gained 1741 yards that season and scored 29 TDs. His career yardage was 3389.

The careers of Haden and McKay, who (oddly) were both 5′ 11″ tall and 170 pounds, continued to be intertwined. They matriculated at Southern Cal (of course) where they starred for John McKay's Rose Bowl teams.

* * *

Some other passing feats:

Don Bowden, at Kathleen High, Lakeland, Florida, threw 91 touchdown passes in 1967–70. Joe Ferguson, Woodlawn High, Shreveport, Louisiana, who threw 86 as a prep, tops the list of single-season yardage gainers with 3293 in 1968.

Quarterbacks at West Side High, Smithfield,

Virginia, tossed a total of 11 scoring strikes in a 124-0 victory in 1967.

The one-game high-school touchdown passing record is believed to be held by Jimmy Hogan, Newport News (Virginia) High, who had nine in a game in 1967. He was going for his tenth as he drove his team to the opponents' 5-yard line but he couldn't get another timeout. If Hogan doesn't hold the one-game mark, he must hold the back-to-back record. The next week he threw seven more scoring strikes.

Thomas Caught 13 Clutch Passes
In The Final Quarter Of His Big Game

"Down and out" is a pass receiver's pattern. But on October 28, 1972, the term described the mood of one of the great high-school passing combinations of all time. Quarterback Bobby Baker and his pet receiver, Bobby Thomas, were being swamped as their Upper Merion High team of King of Prussia, Pennsylvania, was losing, 18-0, to interleague rival Abbington High. Three quarters of the game between the unbeatens were behind them and a constant downpour dampened Upper Merion's chances of getting back into contention.

For Baker and Thomas, it was a shocking experience. As juniors the year before, Baker had tossed 33 scoring passes and Thomas took 18 of them over the goal line. As seniors, they were on their way to High School All-America honors. Baker would end up with a two-year total of 5316 yards (on 348 completions in 583 attempts) and Thomas 2738 yards (on 182 receptions). In all, Thomas had 213 catches for 47 TDs during his brilliant three-year varsity career.

In fact, earlier in the 1972 season, Thomas had caught 23 passes in a single game against William Tennent High for what may be a national prep record. At least it was better than the NFL and NCAA records, even though the high-school game is only 48 minutes long.

But in the downpour of that later October game, with their unbeaten season on the line, Baker and Thomas were mere mortals. Abbington had intercepted Baker six times and returned two for touchdowns in the early going. At the end of three periods, Thomas had caught only four passes.

With such a fine aerial combination, though, there was only one way to get back into the game. Coach Frank Murphy instructed his team to pass every time it got the ball. The strategy may not have worked in the third quarter, but it did in the fourth.

Baker got Upper Merion on the scoreboard with a TD pass to one of his other receivers after Thomas helped set it up with a couple of dazzling catches. Then in the final 4 minutes he began going to his 5′ 9″, 160-pound flanker. Baker-to-Thomas set up another TD on the 3-yard line. Upper Merion then scored on what would be their only running play in the second half. That made the score 24-13, Abbington.

Upper Merion got the ball again after recovering an onside kick on Abbington's 38. Thomas, who would later be clocked at near 4.4 speed in the 40 at the University of Nebraska, sprinted straight downfield on a fly pattern. As he got to the end zone, the ball was zeroing in on him. But so were two Abbington players. All three went up into the air. As Murphy recalled later, after viewing the game films, Thomas remained suspended in the air after the other two had hit the ground. Thomas caught the ball. After the extra point, Upper Merion trailed only 24-20.

Again Upper Merion recovered an onside kick. And again it went to Thomas. Two plays later, the speed receiver took a short swing pass and dashed 52 yards for another TD. Upper Merion had tallied three TDs in 89 seconds. It won the game, 27-24, and kept its unbeaten string intact.

When statisticians figured up that final quarter, they credited Thomas with 13 catches—and 17 for the game, for a total of 213 yards. Not bad for a rainy day.

* * *

Another great explosion by a pass receiver happened in 1969, when Pete Demmerle of New Caanan (Connecticut) High was playing in his state's championship game. Demmerle, who had caught as many as 18 passes in a game, scored four touchdowns within a 4:26-minute period of the title game. His receptions that year accounted for 114 of New Caanan's points.

Four years later, as a junior at Notre Dame, Demmerle again put forth a clutch performance, making the key catch in the Irish's drive for the winning field goal against Alabama. Notre Dame won the 1973 national championship as a result.

Kapp's 7 Touchdown Passes In One NFL Game

More than one pro football quarterback shares the NFL record of seven touchdown passes in a single game. But if ever there was an unlikely candidate for the record, it had to be the Minnesota Vikings' Joe Kapp in 1969.

Four players had accomplished the feat before Kapp stepped onto the field against the Baltimore Colts on September 28, 1969. Their names were Sid Luckman, Adrian Burk, George Blanda and Y. A. Tittle, names that were synonymous with the passing game. Joe Kapp? His passes wobbled sometimes and floated other times, and most of the time he got to play because of his bullish way of driving a football team downfield. He made a career out of threatening to run, then dropping off dinky passes to wide-open receivers. He was more adapted to the Canadian Football League style of play, which he had spent most of his professional career doing.

The ex-California star left the Canadian League for the NFL when he was 29 years old. He seemed ideal for frigid Minnesota. Yet the Viking fans, hungry for a winner, were cool to him. For much of 1967 and 1968, he played amidst the boos of his own "followers." In 1968, he threw only 10 TD passes.

Joe Kapp sat the bench at the start of the 1969 season. He got to play in game No. 2 against the defending NFL champion Baltimore Colts only because the Vikings were displeased with their quarterbacking and as usual returned to gutsy Injun Joe, who at least was a field leader.

Injun Joe went on a rampage.

He completed his first six passes of the game. One of those was to Dave Osborn, a back, when the game was hardly two minutes old. The Osborn pass was good for 18 yards and a touchdown. Soon after, he launched a bomb to end Gene Washington, who strode 83 yards for another TD.

In the next period, Kapp threw scoring strikes of 21 yards to wide receiver Bob Grim and 13 to tight end Kent Kramer.

Then in the third quarter, he iced the game away with TD throws to Washington again, for 41 yards, and another tight end, John Beasley, for 1 yard.

Finally in the fourth quarter, he found yet another receiver for his seventh and record-tying touchdown—running back Dale Lindsey. Kapp got off a 15-yarder to him to bring the final score to 52-14, Vikings. It was the second worst defeat in the Colts' glorious history.

Ironically, one of the men whose record Kapp tied was in the crowd that day. In fact, Adrian Burk had the best "seat" in the house. He was the official backfield judge.

All in all, Kapp struck for 449 yards that day, another Viking record. And he did it in his usual maverick fashion—hitting 12 different receivers for what may be another record.

Despite his record start, Kapp did not finish among the league's top passers that season. Again, he was only tenth. But when the Super Bowl arrived, there was ol' Injun Joe, somehow completing his passes against the Kansas City Chiefs.

Fears Caught 18 Passes
In One NFL Game

There was no question that Tom Fears was going to be a star the moment he came into the National Football League in 1948. That season, the UCLA grad caught 51 passes for the Los Angeles Rams to lead the league. In the ensuing years, Fears would have a lot of things going for him—two standout quarterbacks in Bob Waterfield and Norm Van Brocklin and a dazzling receiving mate, Elroy Hirsch, to take the pressure off him. But Fears made the best of his opportunities.

For three straight seasons, he led the NFL in receptions. As a second-year man he had 77 catches, to break the pro record set by the immortal Don Hutson of Green Bay. Fears may not have set the world afire after he caught the ball, especially in comparison to Crazylegs Hirsch, but he did his job and helped the Rams achieve their victories in some of their most glorious years.

As a third-year man in 1950, Fears again had a chance to lead the league as the team prepared for its final game. In fact, with 66 catches going into the December 3 game with Green Bay, he had an outside chance of matching his league record.

The Rams had the divisional title wrapped up at the time, so they could afford to play around with their potential record breakers. Waterfield would work the first and final quarters and Van Brocklin would pitch the ball in between.

"In some cases, it is very hard for a receiver to adjust to two different quarterbacks," Fears explained about the dual-passing situation. "But in the case of Waterfield and Van Brocklin, there really was no significant problem. Both were excellent passers and it made it easy for the receiver."

As it turned out, the game became a pushover for the powerful Rams, and there would be time to get Fears his record if he were up to the assignment.

Fears caught six passes in the first half of the game. In the third period he caught two more. That put him within reach of his own NFL record of 77 so the Rams rallied behind him for the fourth period. He would only need three more to tie and four to break his mark.

As Fears recalled, "The guys knew I had a big

day going for me so they sort of fed me the ball in the final quarter. There was nothing to be lost by it and the passes to me continued to click." Not only did Fears get his three or four, but the 6′ 3″, 215-pound tight end started cutting to the middle of the defense behind the line and grabbed several quick passes. He had more than enough for the record. From there, he began going through his usual mixture of patterns, and Waterfield continued to find him.

Fears caught 10 passes in the fourth quarter alone, bringing his total for the day to 18—four over the NFL record. He also had upped his season mark to 84, a record which stood until 1964.

The Rams won the game, 51-14, so nothing was lost in treating the team's ace receiver to record performance. Little did the Rams know, however, that the record would hold for years to come. Only Sonny Randle of the St. Louis Cardinals in 1962, with 16, has even come close. Fears had almost that many in the second half alone of an obscure game back in 1950.

KICKING

Rechichar Set An NFL Field-Goal Record On His First Try As A Professional

After Tom Dempsey of the New Orleans Saints catapulted a 63-yard field goal in 1970 to wipe out Bert Rechichar's 17-year-old National Football League record, Rechichar was one of the first people to offer his congratulations. "I was glad to see him do it," said Rechichar, who by then had retired from the game and was back home in Bell Vernon, Pennsylvania. "Tom has accomplished a great feat. Besides, he has that bad foot and a withered hand. I'm glad someone like him was able to do it."

Dempsey had been born with physical handicaps, yet he courageously made it to pro football despite the problems. But Dempsey, who kicked regularly in the pros, was one of the modern day "specialists"—the men who command good salaries for just kicking the football.

Rechichar had come into the league as an all-around player, and mostly as a defensive back. At the University of Tennessee, Rechichar had been a standout. Among his many feats at Knoxville, he had booted a 47-yard field goal against Vanderbilt, as well as four other three-pointers. But he was drafted by the Cleveland Browns in 1952, and that team just happened to have a kicker named Lou (The Toe) Groza, who ruled the pro football placement kickers for many years. Rechichar wasn't in demand as a defensive either by the championship Brown teams. So he was traded to the Baltimore Colts the following spring.

Again Rechichar found himself being upstaged as a kicker—this time by ex-Oklahoma star Buck McPhail. Rechichar did make the Colts as a defensive back, though.

Then on September 27, 1953, with the Colts playing the defensive-minded Chicago Bears, McPhail was sent out to try a field goal with only seconds remaining on the first-half clock. For some reason, though, Coach Weeb Ewbank of the Colts had a hunch that Rechichar would kick the ball further and thus prevent the Bears from getting in field position to score. With three seconds to go, Rechichar was asked if he could give it a try. He had already removed his helmet and was on his way to the dressing room. He muttered something to the effect, "Aw, what the heck, why not," and he went into the game and told his holder Tom Keene to place the ball down quickly, because he would need all the time he could get.

Then Rechichar slammed his foot into the ball for the first time in a pro game. It traveled 56 yards and cleared the uprights, much to the surprise of the kicker himself.

Rechichar had broken Lou Groza's record!

The rugged defensive back would be called upon for other long-distance kicks in the future and would respond with 54- and 53-yarders. But nothing was better than the first one, in terms of distance or incredibility.

Pro Record-Holder Dempsey Also Kicked
A Long Field Goal Without His Shoe On

Tom Dempsey became a national celebrity on November 8, 1970, when he lofted a 63-yard field goal over the defensive line of the Detroit Lions. It gave the New Orleans Saints a badly needed victory and it gave Dempsey the National Football League distance record by a full 7 yards. Dempsey had been crippled from birth with one size 3 foot and the other size 10½. He also had a withered arm.

But at 263 powerful pounds and a keen desire to make the pros, Dempsey became one of the league's great folk heroes. Even after he lost his job with the Saints, he showed the determination needed to make it back to the NFL. After he came back—in 1971—he led the Philadelphia Eagles and the NFL in percentage with 12 of 17.

Like many field-goal kickers, Dempsey did

some of his most amazing feats in practice, kicking 65 yards at random.

He once made a field goal in a semipro game, though, that must rank alongside his NFL record boot in interest. After he got out of Palomar Junior College, he played on a weekend team in hopes of catching on with a regular pro team. In one of those semi-pro games, he kicked a 57-yarder—without a shoe.

*   *   *

Distance kickers get all the credit, naturally, but here are some other NFL field goal "feets":

Most consecutive field goals: 16, by Jan Stenerud, Kansas City Chiefs, 1969.

Most field goals made in a game: 7, by Jim Bakken, St. Louis Cardinals, vs. Pittsburgh Steelers, September 24, 1967 (He attempted 9, which is another record).

Most consecutive games kicking field goals: 31, by Fred Cox, Minnesota Vikings, 1968-70.

Most field goals in a season: 34, by Jim Turner, New York Jets, 1968.

Highest completion percentage in a season (minimum: 14 attempts): 88.5, by Lou Groza, Cleveland Browns, 1953, who made good on 23 of 26.

Peters Kicked 17 Field Goals
During A College Freshman Game

The fans at the Montana State–Billings Tech freshman football game on November 1, 1924 had to figure something strange was going on when the Montana State yearling star, Frosty Peters, stopped short of a touchdown on purpose. Peters had broken away from the Billings defense and raced untouched toward the goal. But as he got within 10 yards, he halted and casually drop-kicked the ball through the uprights. His potential six-point touchdown had suddenly become a three-pointer.

The Montana State coach seemed unperturbed, however, at the tactics of his star back. Right away the crowd figured Peters had his coach's blessings.

The antics continued the next time Montana State got the ball, as a pass receiver stopped short of the goal line in what clearly was a scoring situation. On the next play Peters drop-kicked his second three-pointer.

Peters wasn't so accurate for the rest of the half, but his teammates, obviously tuned in to the record-breaking strategy, did all they could to help against hapless Billings Tech. Twelve more times in the half, Peters got to try drop kicks; seven more times he made them.

In the second half, the strange pattern continued, with Montana State more interested in Peters' quest for a national record (a high-school player had made 15 in 1915) than it was in touchdowns.

Even Peters got on the ball. He made eight of eight in little over a quarter, bringing his total to 17 of 22. With Montana State leading, 51-0, Peters left the game and the team was allowed to go for touchdowns. Later the Montana State coach admitted that the game was a setup for Peters and a record attempt.

Strangely enough, the game may have cost Montana State the services of Peters. Illinois coach Bob Zuppke heard about the feat and summoned the star to the Champaign campus. Peters obliged and never played for Montana State again.

At Illinois, there was no time for such gimmicks, and Peters would never again be involved in a record-setting situation. Besides, he had to share the glory there. In his backfield in 1925 was a halfback named Red Grange, who was setting some records of his own.

Caputo Kicked A 60-Yard Field Goal For A National High-School Record

Ross Caputo was following his coach's instructions when he lined up to attempt a 60-yard field goal for Judge Memorial Catholic High School of Salt Lake City, Utah. As Coach Gil Cordova would say later, "We were just trying to kick to put Hillcrest High in the hole." What Caputo wound up doing was to put Judge Memorial in the lead, 3-0, with his amazing field goal on September 4, 1970. The NCAA record for a field goal at the time was only 59 yards. The NFL record was 56.

Before Caputo lined up for his record boot on a windswept Friday night in 1970, he had kicked only two field goals and his percentage had been poor. He wasn't even his team's regular kicker the year before, and his best in a game was a 35-yarder as a sophomore in 1968.

The 5' 7", 180-pounder had learned to kick

under his father, who once booted for Utah State. The son became a good technician. As he recalled his record kick, he said his coach gave the order because a 35-mile gale would have sent a punt into the end zone, requiring it to be brought back to the 20. The coach figured a field goal would fall short of the goal line and put the Hillcrest team in a bind.

"I knew it was going a long way as soon as I put my foot in it," Caputo told reporters later. "I kick the lower 25 per cent of the ball and this time it was a slush connection. It really sailed out. It went end-over-end and seemed to catch in a windstream because it just kept going and going. It went over the crossbar with room to spare."

As it turned out, the three-point kick was all the scoring for the night. But the kick, not the victory, was the talk of the day.

In all the excitement, the official statistician reported that it was a 64-yard kick and that story went across the nation through the Associated Press. A confused Salt Lake City reporter or typesetter printed that it was kicked from the "51 (*sic*) yard line," of which there is none, of course. But the Judge Memorial coach double-checked, and reset the record from 64 to 60.

* * *

Before Caputo set his mark, the longest field goal on record by a high-school player was 59.

That record, set by Bill Phelps of Colorado Springs High School, was set in a game at Florence, Colorado, in 1923. Phelps' record, in a way, may pass the test of time even longer than Caputo's; it was a drop kick!

Braswell Made All Of His Extra Points During His High-School Career

There are three parts that go into a successful extra point—the snap from the center, the correct positioning by the holder, and the kick itself. To get that right combination week after week and year after year in high-school football seems outright impossible.

Kim Braswell of Avondale (Georgia) High School found the knack, however. During his four-year career, from 1965 through 1968, he made 134 out of 134 attempts.

As a senior he also was three-for-three on field goals, booting from the 43, the 38 and the 33.

Braswell was lucky. He had a center named Flem Mitchell who had snapped the ball for him from grammar-school days. He also played for a high scoring team. But a player who goes 134-for-134 is more than lucky. He's downright good.

The Davis Brothers Scored 471 Points On Kicks For The University Of Alabama

When Paul (Bear) Bryant was a young assistant coach at the University of Alabama in the 1930s, the first player he ever recruited was a youngster named Alvin (Pig) Davis. Davis played for some good teams that had a combined 16-2-1 record and contributed three touchdowns to the Crimson Tide during his stay at Tuscaloosa. Then he went on to become a very successful high-school coach in Columbus, Georgia. Bryant went on to other coaching successes, too —at Maryland, Kentucky and Texas A&M. But when The Bear got back to Tuscaloosa as head coach in the 1950s, he sought out his old protégé, Davis, for some high-school prospects.

Davis sent Alabama several standouts but the three he will be remembered best for were his own sons—Tim, Steve and Bill. Unlike their father, none of the three ever scored a touchdown for the Crimson Tide. But among them, they scored a total of 471 points as kickers.

With a Davis kicking for the varsity in all but three seasons from 1961 through 1973, the Tide won 90 games, lost only 10 and tied two—and never was shutout. Each Davis player participated in a maximum of three bowl games. Then all three went on to Alabama's medical school, since they were virtually straight-A students.

Tim, who played during 1961–63, overcame a knee injury and banged in a total of 139 points on conversions and field goals as a three-year starter. His four FGs gave Alabama a 12-7 victory over Ole Miss in the 1964 Sugar Bowl game to offset the loss of Joe Namath, who was suspended for the contest.

Next came Steve, 1965–67, who got a late start because as a sophomore he served only as the team's punter. But he still managed to score 112 points in his final two seasons.

Bill, who was the Tide's regular kicker in 1971–73, turned out to be the finest of them all. He kicked 75 points to tie the NCAA record as a sophomore and matched his own record in his senior year. He had another record—211 points on kicks—in regular season play (the NCAA does not count bowl statistics) and 220 points overall.

For the record, here's how the Davis brothers did individually during their careers:

Kicking

| | Regular Season | | Bowl Games | |
	P.A.T.	FG	P.A.T.	FG
Tim	77–67	29–17	3–3	7–6
Steve	47–44	31–18	5–5	3–3
Bill	143–133	40–26	3–2	2–2
Totals	267–244	100–61	11–10	12–11

Unfortunately, for all their kicking feats, the reign of the three Davis brothers did not have a happy conclusion. Bill, who kicked a 46-yard field goal (his longest ever) to help beat Southern Cal in his varsity debut, missed his final extra point on New Year's Eve, 1973. The kick went wide right in the Sugar Bowl game and left Alabama leading Notre Dame, 23-21, in a contest that would decide the national title. Notre Dame roared back up field in the waning moments of the game and got the winning field goal.

But there would be an opportunity for redemption. Back in Tuscaloosa, another Davis, freshman numeral winner Mike, was waiting in the wings.

O'Neal Punted 98 Yards In An NFL Game

One could say that Steve O'Neal came into the National Football League with a boom during his rookie season.

As a collegian at Texas A&M, O'Neal had averaged about 42 yards per punt during his three-year varsity career. There was nothing special to earmark him for pro football stardom, though. He had had a 73-yard kick, but that came while he was a sophomore, and most punters will get off a long one sooner or later if they kick often. To the defending world champion New York Jets, he was worth a 13th-round draft choice—the 338th player taken in the 1969 talent pool.

The Jets weren't too pleased with their regular punter, Curley Johnson, and O'Neal was afforded the chance to beat him out. O'Neal made a 38-yard kick in the College All-Star game and went on to earn himself a job even though he did

Incredible Football Feats

Ken Hall: In 1953, as a senior at Sugar Land (Texas) High School, Hall scored 395 points.

Billy Johnson (right) not only set the college record for long-distance touchdowns, but also broke the record of 246.3 "all-purpose" yards set by Colorado's "Whizzer" White, now Supreme Court Justice Byron R. White (left).

Wilbert Montgomery scored 37 touchdowns as a college freshman. His helmet carries a star for each one.

George Blanda holds all-time scoring records for 3 professional football teams. On October 31, 1971 (left) he scored 8 points, bringing his career total to 1609, for a new all-time pro football scoring record. Going into 1974, he had 1842.

3

In 1934 Beattie Feathers set an NFL record for yards per rush that still stands: 9.4 yards per carry.

On December 16, 1973, O.J. Simpson topped 2000 yards rushing to smash the NFL mark set by Jim Brown (right) a decade earlier.

Harry Newman, the quarterback who on November 11, 1934 set a record of 38 carries in one game. It stood until 1973.

Eric "the Flea" Allen. This 5'9", 161-pound back gained 350 yards rushing for Michigan State, October 30, 1971.

6

On October 12, 1968, Bruce Swanson (12) of North Park College threw 10 TD passes against North Central College for an all-time single-game college record. North Park's receiver, Paul Zaeske (82), scored 8 TDs in the same game—a record that may last longer than Swanson's.

7

Tom Fears, who on December 3, 1950, caught 18 passes for the L.A. Rams against Green Bay, for the NFL record.

On his first try as a pro, September 27, 1953, Bert Rechichar set an NFL record for longest field goal (56 yards).

Jets rookie Steve O'Neal punted 98 yards on September 21, 1969, to break a 45-year-old NFL record.

Blocking a field goal at the crossbar—R.C. Owens, December 8, 1962.

Ken Houston of the Houston Oilers set a pro record with 4 interception returns for TD's in 1971.

In 1948, his first year ever as a head coach, Bennie Oosterbaan led the University of Michigan to a 9-0-0 season and a national championship.

Coach Paul "Bear" Bryant led the University of Alabama to 15 straight bowl games.

William M. Heston, the greatest star of Michigan's Point-A-Minute Teams, which in 1901-1905 scored 2821 points in 57 games for an average of 49.5 an outing.

On December 8, 1940, the Chicago Bears won the NFL Championship by an astounding 73-0 victory over the Redskins. Here George McAfee (5) slides off tackle to pick up seven yards.

Pat Palinkas (3) of the Orlando Panthers (Atlantic Coast Football League), the first woman to play pro football, holding the ball for Panthers' place-kicker Steve Palinkas (her husband).

In 1972, fourteen-year-old Tony Capozzoli had a completion percentage of .59, gained 455 yards on 63 carries, punted for a 41.4-yard average (higher than 16 regular NFL punters') and kicked 3 field goals and 27 of 29 extra points.

Doak Walker. In 1955 the Detroit Lions halfback figured in all ten of the NFL's statistical categories.

15

Six of the seven Nesser brothers who played for the old Columbus Panhandles in the early 1900's. Left to right: Ted, John, Phil, Al, Frank, and Fred.

Bob Hayes, "King of the Hill" among pro football's speed demons. In 1973 he ran a 4.3 40 for a pro *track* record.

16

not show much more than Johnson in preseason drills.

O'Neal pretty much went unnoticed in the Jets' league opener. But then again, punters usually get little attention unless they muff a kick at a crucial time. In his second game, at mile-high Denver, he would get a better opportunity to show his stuff. The rarefied air at that altitude is a kicker's delight.

The NFL record going into the September 21st Jet–Bronco game was 94, set by a tackle named Wilbur Henry almost 46 years before. Henry played for the old Canton Bulldogs in an era when the football was shaped more like today's volleyballs and punting was an integral part of football strategy. The 6′ 3″, 185-pound O'Neal could not begin to match the 245-pound "Fats" Henry's launching power, either. The best kick with a modern football was 90 yards by Don Chandler of the 1965 Green Bay Packers. And Bobby Scarpitto had lifted one 87 yards for Denver at Denver in 1968.

But O'Neal was more concerned with holding a job than holding a record when the Jets went to Denver. The Jets were on their own 1-yard line when O'Neal came into the game.

Standing behind the goal line, O'Neal got off the greatest punt in pro football history. He had only a 5-mph wind in his favor. But the ball sailed over 70 yards and bounded near the Denver 30-yard line, where ace kick-returner Bill

Thompson tried for a running over-the shoulder catch. Thompson missed and the ball bounced down to the 1-yard line, where it stopped. Thompson managed a 1-yard return.

Officially, the ball traveled 98 yards, from the 1 to the other 1. You can't do any better than that and keep the ball inbounds.

The punt came out of nowhere and caught the statisticians and other experts by surprise, so there was no actual measurement as to how far the ball traveled through the air. But estimates by those on the scene say it may have gone as far as 77 yards if one counts the distance behind the goal line to where O'Neal kicked.

O'Neal's record blast did not turn out to be a "shot heard round the world"—even the football world. It got surprisingly little play in the New York papers, his toe being upstaged by Joe Namath's injured rib. And for the year, O'Neal would finish only fourth in the 13-team American Football Conference. But he left a record that would be hard to match.

* * *

It was late in the third quarter of a meaningless exhibition game on August 11, 1962, and the Green Bay Packers led the Dallas Cowboys, 24-7. The Cowboys' predicament was made worse when they were forced into a punting situation.

And the situation seemed even worse when

Sam Baker, the team's punter, fumbled the ball. As the world champion Packers began closing in on him, Baker picked up the ball and got off the best kick he could.

Baker got a good foot into the ball. It landed and then began to roll. And roll. And roll.

All together, the punt traveled over 100 yards, into the end zone.

Officially, he got credit for an 85-yard punt, undoubtedly the longest one ever made in a pro game after a fumble.

Bateman Averaged 52.7 Yards On His Punts And Had A 46-Yard Field Goal The Same Day

The year 1971 was a good one for the University of Utah's Marv Bateman. While setting a national record for best punting (48.1), the rangy kicker got off 30 punts that sailed over 50 yards. In four separate games, he averaged over 50 yards as a punter.

Bateman reached his zenith, though, in an October 30 game against the University of Wyoming.

The day was near freezing but Bateman was hot. Six of his seven punts traveled 52 yards or more. The longest was 62. The average was 52.7. More important, the booming punts were not returned very far, as long punts often are. Wyoming's runback aces could only haul the seven punts back for a total of 38 yards. Bateman had gained 338 yards in field position on his opponents.

To top off his fine performance, Bateman skyrocketed a 46-yard field goal that was good.

Otherwise, October 30 was glum. Utah lost the game, 29-16.

DEFENSE

Owens Blocked A Field Goal At The Crossbar

They called him "Alley Oop" because of his unique style of catching the looping passes that quarterback Y. A. Tittle lofted to him in their days together with the San Francisco 49ers. R. C. Owens was pro football's greatest leaper. He earned that reputation after first proving it in two other sports. At the University of Idaho, Owens had once led the nation with an astonishing 27.6-per-game rebounding average, and he high jumped almost 7 feet.

It didn't take his pro football teammates long to appreciate his bounding talents. But one teammate, star place-kicker Tommy Davis, was kidding R. C. one day as they watched game films of a Detroit Lion kick narrowly clearing the crossbar on a 50-yard field goal. "You could have gotten that once, R. C." said Davis that day in 1960. Owens agreed.

The crossbar in football is 10 feet high, the same as the rim in basketball. And R. C. had blocked enough shots and gone above the rim for enough rebounds in his time at Idaho. So he approached 49er Coach Red Hickey and asked if he could give it a try. Hickey said no.

The 6′ 3″, 190-pound Owens didn't give up on his dream, though.

When he was traded to the Baltimore Colts in 1962, he approached Head Coach Weeb Ewbank with the same proposition. The two figured that it was worth a try, even if only for the psychological effect it might have on a kicker. Besides, the Colts needed a deep man to run back kicks in case the field goals fell short, and R. C. was a good man in the open field.

Owens began practicing the leap to perfect his technique. He finally got to try it in a game against his old 49er teammates. Fans looked on in disbelief as R. C. lined up underneath the goal post. But the kick fell short and Plan B went into effect. R. C. ran the ball back from the 2 to the midfield stripe. Later in the season, Bob Khayat of the Washington Redskins teed up the ball on the 40 for a fairly long attempt and R. C. again meandered in front of the crossbar like a soccer goalie. As Khayat's kick descended toward the crossbar, R. C. carefully timed his leap—and *oomph* . . . in true Alley Oop fashion tipped the ball away.

Alley Oop had proved his point.

Ironically, the game was on national television, and not too long after Owens heard from another basketball player who said he might be interested in joining a pro team as a possible field goal blocker. The player's name was Wilt Chamberlain.

Suffridge Blocked 3 Sammy Baugh Punts In A Single Pro Football Game

Along with being one of the greatest passers of all time, Slingin' Sammy Baugh of the Washington Redskins also was the premier punter in pro football history. His kicking deeds are found in many places in the National Football League record book. Sammy holds the marks for best punting average in a game (minimum 4 punts) with 59.4 yards in a 1940 game; best average in a season with 51.3; and best average in a career with 44.93. He punted often in his 16 years as a professional, and once punted 14 times in a single game.

But there was a time when punter Baugh met his match on the professional field. The adversary was a rookie lineman out of the University of Tennessee named Bob Suffridge. The newcomer was no ordinary rookie. He has been considered as an all-time All-America guard out of the days when football players had to go both ways.

In a late 1941 game, when neither team was going anywhere in the standings, Baugh's Washington Redskins met Suffridge's Philadelphia Eagles. That day Bob Suffridge broke through three times to block Sammy Baugh punts. Though it didn't make the record books and it didn't save the Eagles from a 20-14 defeat, Suffridge's achievement has to be unequalled in pro football history.

Unfortunately for the rookie, though, history affected his achievement in more ways than one that day. Bob Suffridge chose December 7, the day World War II broke out, to accomplish his unusual feat. The newspapers had little inclination to report the performance the following day.

Foley Scored 2 TDs On Blocked Punts During An NFL Game

The National Football League record book has hundreds of categories. Before the start of the 1973 season, there were 203 categories for individual all-time performances alone.

On November 11, 1973, Tim Foley of the Miami Dolphins created a new subhead in the record books: "Misc. TDs, 2 in 1 game." The NFL, for all its planning, had not allowed for a man who would score twice after blocked punts in one game. Only once had a man scored two TDs that way in one season; it happened 16 years before Foley was born.

In 1973, the Dolphins were playing their intra-divisional rival, the Baltimore Colts, for the second time when Foley broke through in the opening period and blocked Bruce Lee's punt on the 18-yard line. Foley scrambled for the loose ball and got it at the 8, then simply ran it in for his first TD.

Later in the game, his teammate, linebacker Bob Matheson, got to the veteran punter on the 14-yard line and blocked his kick. This time, Foley picked up the ball on the 5 and ran it in again.

The Dolphins won the game, 44-0.

For a rugged 6', 194-pounder who had started three years for the high-scoring Dolphins, it was an unusual way to break into the scoring columns for the first time.

McIntire Scored 3 TDs In A Game After Recovering Opponents' Fumbles

Defensive end Kenny McIntire of South High in Parkersburg, West Virginia, wasn't very big. But on October 2, 1971, his opponents thought he stood pretty tall.

That day, McIntire turned three miscues by the Toledo (Ohio) DeVilbiss High School team's backs into scoring bursts of his own.

McIntire grabbed fumbles and ran them back for 24, 35 and 36 yards. In the short run, his efforts helped South High defeat DeVilbiss, 48-14. In the long run, he would earn All-State honors.

Brosky Averaged Over One Interception
A Game In His College Career

Al Brosky liked to look into a quarterback's eyes as he played defensive back for the University of Illinois in the early 1950s. Then, as the passer would release the ball, Brosky would scoot in with all his speed and daring and swipe the ball. It was a proven formula: in three years and 25 games for the Illini, Brosky intercepted a record 29 passes.

Brosky intercepted three passes in his very first college game.

At one point in his career, the 5' 11", 170-pounder filched passes in 15 straight games. Twice he intercepted 10 passes in a season. He was, by any standard, the best pass thief ever to play the college game.

A Chicagoan, Brosky knew what to do with the ball when he got it, too. He had several runbacks of 30 yards or more and one scoring burst of 61. In another tough game, he had two intercepts in his own end zone.

Two decades after his career ended in 1952, no other collegian has come within nine interceptions of Brosky's record total, even though college players were throwing more than ever before.

Houston Set A Pro Record
With 4 Interception Returns For TDs

The Houston Oilers had a difficult time winning football games in the late 1960s and early 1970s. Their few successes in that time were due in part to a guy named Houston—defensive back Ken Houston.

A record nine times in his career, Ken Houston ran back interceptions for touchdowns. The last two of those scoring bursts came in a single game, against the San Diego Chargers. Like most of Houston's other runbacks after snatching balls out of the air, that too was a National Football League record.

In each of the eight games where Ken Houston intercepted passes and returned them for scores, his team avoided defeat. The first time they fought to a tie, but after that his dazzling returns spelled victories.

Ken Houston was a hit during his first season

in the league (1967) which was amazing because
the 6′ 3″ safetyman from Lufkin, Texas, never
played in the secondary until he reached the pros.
He had been a small middle linebacker in college
at Prairie View A&M. But he adapted quickly
and turned in one scoring runback as a rookie.
That was 1967.

He continued to accumulate interceptions with
regularity from then on, but in 1971 he had the
year that other defensive backs merely dream of.
He was only 27 at the time.

But he had the savvy of a veteran.

"You have to plan the return," he said while
being honored for his triple-crown season of 1971
—most TD returns in a game, in a season, in a
career. "You have to think touchdown all the
way. I want to get my interceptions on the side-
line and head for the middle of the field. That
gets the flow started. And when it's nicely under-
way, when everybody on both teams is sprinting
for the center of the field, that's the time to cut
back. If you are lucky, you can go."

Somebody said that a man who returns four
interceptions for touchdowns in a season is more
than lucky, though. Most quarterbacks in the
NFL would agree to that.

Dryer Nailed 2 Pro QBs For Safeties Within 5 Minutes In One Game

Fred Dryer of the Los Angeles Rams is known for his unusual lifestyle. A California nature lover, Dryer lives where he's at at any given moment. His home is a van. When he goes to work, he's all business, though. The Green Bay Packer quarterbacking corps found that out on October 21, 1973.

The 6′ 6″, 240-pound Ram lineman was tearing apart the Packers to the delight of 80,558 partisans at Los Angeles Coliseum. The ransacking would be so devastating that the Packers would gain only 35 yards rushing and 28 passing during the afternoon.

Dryer admittedly had an edge on the Packers. Their regular offensive tackle—the man entrusted to block Dryer—was out of action and Green Bay had to move a guard into the important position.

Dryer was quick to take advantage of the situation all day long. But in the final period, with the Packers trying desperately to pass their way back into the game, Dryer delivered the all-time insult.

With about 11 minutes to play, he put on a hard outside rush and charged toward Packer quarterback Scott Hunter who was trying to set up in the end zone. Dryer "blind-sided" him, forcing a two-point safety.

The frustrated Packers replaced Hunter with Jim Del Gaizo the next time they got the ball.

So five minutes after Dryer's first safety, he put on another hard outside rush and smacked Del Gaizo head on in the end zone, too. It sealed a 24-7 victory for the Rams.

In the 54 years that the National Football League had been in existence, only six teams had ever scored two safeties in a single game. Only four times had the same player recorded two safeties in a whole season. Yet Dryer matched those feats in five minutes' time in one game.

The 27-year-old Dryer had already corralled another halfback in the end zone in the 1969 season. Thus he came up with another record— three safeties in a career.

Green Did Not Play College Football But Played 170 Straight Games As A Pro

The Dallas Cowboys were only two years old in 1962 when they signed a player who was newer to the game than they were. The Cowboys decided to give a prominent college basketball player from Utah State a chance to make their team as a free agent.

The Cowboys, who had been losing regularly, figured they had nothing further to lose by signing Cornell Green, a three-time All-Skyline Conference cager. At 6' 3" and about 200 pounds, he had the size and speed of a gridiron star even if he didn't have the experience. The Cowboys and Green matured together.

From an inconspicuous start in which he had to defend against All-Pro flanker Boyd Dowler of the World Champion Green Bay Packers, Cornell Green began writing one of the amazing records in pro football. If Green was green, his head was clear as he tackled one of the toughest transitions an athlete with no experience can make—playing cornerback against seasoned and speedy flankers. "You come into the league and everybody has it all to learn anyway, whether they know it or not," he said.

Green just happened to learn faster than the others.

He earned himself a place on the Cowboy team in 1962 and never lost his job. Though he played cornerback and safety—positions where injuries are common—he lasted for 170 games in a row. His streak was intact going into the 1974 season.

As the Cowboys became better and better known, Green received his share of the limelight, too. Five times he made the Pro Bowl all-star team, at both cornerback and safety. Four times he made all-pro.

Perhaps nothing showed that he learned the game better than the off-season job the Cowboys found for him: They made him a talent scout.

Catawba College Recovered 4 Straight Onside Kicks

The onside kick is one of football's most interesting plays. The team that kicks off, whether it does so to start a half or put the ball back in play after a touchdown or field goal, needs only to boot the ball 10 yards to make it a free ball. If the kickoff man can squibble the ball just over the line, it enables his teammates to dash across the line and try to recover it. The strategy is a good one for the team that's behind.

There is one problem with the onside kick strategy, however. It usually doesn't work.

But on one Saturday afternoon in 1972, the strategy worked perfectly.

Tiny Catawba College of Salisbury, North Carolina, was losing 33-0 to Carson-Newman College of Jefferson City, Tennessee, so Catawba had nothing to lose in the second half, despite the odds.

Catawba put some of its best ballhawks up front on the kickoff, and sure enough they recovered. Before Carson-Newman could recover from the shock, Catawba players recovered three more in a row. With each recovery, Catawba marched down the field to score. The steals enabled Catawba to control the football for 26 consecutive plays and a total of nearly 15 minutes. Before the contest was over, Catawba recovered a fifth onside kick.

The result of the strange turn of events almost resulted in a turnabout of the score. Somehow Carson-Newman hung in for a 40-34 triumph, though.

COACHING

Oosterbaan Won A National Championship In His First Year As A Head Coach

Bennie Oosterbaan had been good to the University of Michigan as an athlete. During his undergraduate years in the 1920s, he had starred in four sports. He was an All-America in football (Grantland Rice named him to his all-time team) and in basketball. In baseball, it was said he could have jumped right from the campus to the majors. In track he had Olympic potential as a discus thrower. But Oosterbaan wanted no part of professional athletics or the Olympics after his graduation. Instead, he stayed at the Ann Arbor campus to become an assistant football coach.

For two decades, Oosterbaan pretty much stayed in the background, serving three head coaches. During one period, he doubled as the Wolverines' basketball coach, but he was almost as undistinguished there as he was in football—

his teams never topped the .500 mark in nine seasons.

In 1947, under Fritz Crisler, Michigan put together one of the greatest teams of all time. The Wolverines went head-to-head all season long with Notre Dame in the ratings game, switching on and off in the No. 1 spot. The Irish won out in the final poll because they whipped a ranked Southern Cal team, 38-7, in their last game of the season. In those days, the wire service polls did not include bowl results. However, after the Wolverines crushed Southern Cal in the Rose Bowl, 49-0, the Associated Press conducted another— unofficial—poll, and the Wolverines were named the nation's finest team by a 2-to-1 margin. Oosterbaan had been the backfield coach of that 1947 "Mad Magicians" team, an aggregate that scored 394 points in ten games. But it was Crisler, of course, who got the publicity. The veteran head coach was named the national "Coach of the Year." After the season was over, Crisler retired to devote full time to his other position of athletic director. Oosterbaan was named Michigan's new coach for 1948.

Compared to the dynamic, innovative Crisler, Oosterbaan was quiet and low-key. Some people described him as the "big lazy Dutchman." Some said he got his job because he was part of the university's tradition.

Oosterbaan retained only the remnants of the great 1947 team for his coaching debut. Gone were two All-America backs and most of both the offensive and defensive lines. Oosterbaan, who had been an end as a player, rose to the occasion and groomed two sophomores for his halfbacks, a reserve for his fullback and switched another back, Pete Elliott, from halfback to quarterback. He also patched up the lines.

In the opening game of the 1948 season, Michigan beat its cross-state rival, Michigan State, by a 13-7 score. If Oosterbaan were happy to get out of the game with a victory, some of his critics weren't. The year before, Michigan had beaten the Spartans, 55-0. Oosterbaan's opening day was not helped by the fact that Michigan State's coach was Biggie Munn, a former Wolverine assistant who some Michigan people had figured was Crisler's logical successor.

Michigan's youthful team began to jell, though, right after the opener. It would not become the high-scoring juggernaut of the previous year, but as the season wore on the offensive unit began averaging about three touchdowns a game and the defense contributed five shutouts. Week after week, the Wolverines got better and better and they climbed into the No. 1 spot in the polls. They clinched the No. 1 ranking by climaxing their season with a 13-3 triumph over arch-rival Ohio State. The Wolverines were a perfect 9-0-0 for their new coach.

Only once since college football began proclaiming national champions in 1924 had a man led a team to the top in his initial season as head coach of the school. And that lone exception— Matty Bell of the 1935 Southern Methodist team —had been head coach at Texas A&M for several years before getting the SMU position.

Oosterbaan was a first-time head coach in all ways, with no head experience in the high school or college ranks. For his remarkable transition Bennie Oosterbaan was named "Coach of the Year." His feat has never been duplicated.

Alabama Has Been To 15 Straight Bowl Games But Georgia Tech Won 8 Straight

No team in the history of college football has gone "bowling" more often than the University of Alabama.

From New Year's Day, 1926, when the Crimson Tide made an appearance at the Rose Bowl, through New Year's Eve, 1973, when they battled Notre Dame for the national championship in the Sugar Bowl, Alabama has taken part in a record 27 post-season classics.

Alabama has appeared in the Rose Bowl, the Orange Bowl, and the Sugar Bowl six times each; the Cotton Bowl four times; the Liberty Bowl and the Bluebonnet Bowl twice; and the Gator Bowl once. The Tide has been the first team to appear in all of the "Big Four" bowls—the Rose, Sugar, Cotton and Orange. It was the first Southern team to go to the Rose Bowl (1926) and the last non-Big Ten team to oppose the West Coast's representative (1946). Each time Alabama won. Alabama was the first team to play for the national championship in a bowl game (in 1966, after the Associated Press decided to take the bowl games into consideration before making its final tabulation of votes)—and won, beating Nebraska, which had been ranked No. 1 going into the game. Alabama also holds the record for the most points in a bowl game—61 versus Syracuse in the 1953 Orange Bowl. Alabama also has the distinction of being involved in one of bowl game history's most bizarre events; in the 1954 Cotton Bowl, Tide star Tommy Lewis jumped off the bench to tackle Rice's Dicky Moegle, who was en route to a touchdown.

But for all of its bowl achievements, nothing is more impressive than Bear Bryant's coaching feat of taking the Tide to 15 straight bowls from the 1959 Liberty Bowl through the 1973 Sugar Bowl. It broke the stretch of 14 straight bowl appearances by Ole Miss under Johnny Vaught and Bruiser Kinard. Bama beat Ole Miss in their only bowl showdown in 1964.

Meanwhile, Alabama's bowl skein continues into the 1974 football season.

* * *

For all its bowl appearances, Alabama has only a 12-12-3 record to show for its games through the Notre Dame match New Year's Eve, 1973.

One football coach, Bobby Dodd of Georgia Tech, set the most enviable bowl record by winning eight straight post-season matches. No one has come close to wiping out that mark of distinction. Dodd took over the Georgia Tech position in 1945. A year later, his 1946 team went to a now-defunct game called the Oil Bowl and defeated St. Mary's of California, 41-19. The Yellowjackets repeated their bowl success the following year at Miami, defeating Kansas, 20-14, for the Orange Bowl title.

Georgia Tech was out of the post-season games until after the 1951 season. Then the Yellowjackets came back to score triumphs in bowl games for six straight years.

Versaci Coached An Unbeaten High-School Team When He Was Just 19 Years Old

What makes a good football coach? Experience?

Tony Versaci wanted very badly to play college football at the University of Detroit. Tony's father had once been a football hero there, so Tony gave it a try as a wide receiver and defensive back, despite the fact that he weighed only 145 pounds. But in his freshman year he injured his knee and had to give up the game—at least as a player. Not content to be a fan, he began helping out as a part-time assistant at a new school, Divine Child High, while he completed his education. Divine Child was as small as the name implies, with an enrollment of about 250 boys. That was in the late 1950s.

During Tony's second year at the school, the

head coach became ill two days before the opening game. It was obvious that he would have to give up the strenuous job of coaching. A petition was made to the state Board of Education, asking if a 19-year-old college undergraduate could take over the reins at a desperate school. The Board gave Versaci the go-ahead.

That season Divine Child, under its boy wonder, went unbeaten. Was the team surprised? Well, not really. Before the season started, the teenage coach told his teenage players, "We are going to win the championship." And they did.

Versaci proved during the 1960s that his first triumph was not a one-shot affair. In his 11 years at the school, Divine Child lost only nine games. Five times they were state champions and seven times they won Detroit city titles. His little school was knocking off high schools of 6,000 enrollment before he moved on to Michigan State in 1970.

In 1971 Versaci was signed to coach the St. Louis Cardinals' specialty teams. At age 32, he did not set any record for being the youngest coach in the National Football League. But he may have been the youngest NFL coach who never played college football.

TEAM RECORDS

Bedford County Training School
Won 78 Consecutive Games

The football seasons from 1942 through 1949 were good ones for little Bedford County Training School in Shelbyville, Tennessee. The all-black high school won 78 games in a row.

Actually, Bedford County T. S. was tougher than the streak sounds—if that is possible. For the first three years of the streak, no opponent crossed its 50-yard line. For the first 52 games of the skein, no one scored on this remarkable team.. Edward Finley coached the team to its first 75 victories, before moving on to a junior high school in Nashville, where he put together another long streak. He said his biggest margin of victory at Bedford County was 68-0. That was unusual, however. Finley liked to get as many second- and third-stringers into the games as possible in order to have experienced players who could continue the winning streak. There were no big-name All-Americas to come out of the teams that compiled the winning streak, but Finley proudly pointed out that 21 of his former players went on to finish college after getting football scholarships.

The glories of Bedford County Training School and its all-time high-school winning streak are a thing of the past, though. The school has been renamed Harris High. The principal there in 1965, who also coached during the streak, said that his school was having trouble recapturing past fortunes. "The integration problem plagues," he said, noting that other schools have siphoned off his best athletes.

* * *

Bedford's streak has been challenged over the years, first by a team from Braddock, Pennsylvania, that rolled up 56 victories. Somehow, because of its odd name "Training School," the Braddock coach mistook Bedford for a reform school. "I told my boys," he said, "that there was a reason why the Tennessee school had a longer streak—they never lost any of their players." The Braddock streak ended in 1953.

Jefferson City (Missouri) High made a run at the record by rolling up 71 consecutive victories from 1958 through 1966.

Some other notable streaks:

Pittsfield, Illinois (1966–73) 65

Team Records

Colgate Was Undefeated, Untied And Unscored-On In 1932

Undefeated and untied college football teams aren't exactly a dime a dozen. Yet there is at least one every year. Undefeated, untied and unscored-on teams, however, are extinct. In the past half-century there has been only one big-time team that could claim that distinction. And with the current rules that call for longer seasons, wide-open offenses, platoon systems and more plays in a game, the likelihood of seeing another major-college football team with a perfect all-shutout record is remote.

The last team to perform the feat was Colgate, a prominent school in Hamilton, New York, that has become one of the lesser lights in big-time college football. The year was 1932.

The Red Raiders began prepping for their historical season in 1929 when they brought in a brilliant football strategist named Andy Kerr to be head coach. Appropriately his first team scored a shutout in its first game. White-washings became commonplace with Kerr-coached teams. In his first three seasons at Hamilton, the Red Raiders recorded 19 of them in 29 games. Then came 1932.

That year, Kerr assembled a team that he called not physically powerful but "unsurpassed in intelligence." Kerr applied the lessons he had learned as an assistant under the fabled Glenn (Pop) Warner.

In its opener that season, Colgate rolled up 41 points on hapless St. Lawrence University and pushed the opponents all over the field on defense. For its next seven games, the Red Raiders were also as tight as the purse-strings of that Depression year. Opponents weren't even coming close to Colgate's goal line. The season finale, however, was expected to be more of a real test of Colgate's strength. Brown University was bringing in an undefeated team that was pretty good in its own right on defense. The Bruins had given up only 21 points in its first seven games.

Brown threatened to ruin Colgate's unblemished record in the first half as a Bruin back got within inches of the goal line on the final play before the intermission. But he was stymied. In the second half, Colgate's defense stiffened and the Raiders roared back to beat Brown, 21-0.

* * *

In the days that were to follow, Colgate added another "un" to its undefeated, untied, unscored-on record. Surely the Red Raiders would be asked to take part in a post-season bowl game—but they went "uninvited."

Perhaps getting shut out themselves—by the bowls—was a blessing for this remarkable team. In 1938, Duke University went undefeated, untied and unscored-on in the regular season, then had its record tarnished with a 7-3 defeat by Southern Cal in the Rose Bowl. In 1939, Tennessee's greatest team ever was unbeaten, untied and unscored-on, too, in the regular season, only to lose 14-0 in the Rose Bowl. Again the culprit was Southern Cal.

The 1932 Record

Colgate		Opp.
41	St. Lawrence	0
27	Case Tech	0
47	Niagara U.	0
35	Lafayette	0
14	New York U.	0
31	Penn State	0
32	Mississippi College	0
16	Syracuse	0
21	Brown University	0

Michigan's Point-A-Minute Teams

Perhaps no football team in history dominated an era as the University of Michigan's "Point-A-Minute" teams did from 1901 through 1905. For that period, the Wolverines scored a total of 2821 points in 57 games—an average of 49.5 per outing. If they fell short of making a full 60 points per game, they could be excused. Many games were called before regulation time ended in order to spare downtrodden opponents further embarrassment. Furthermore, the touchdowns which Michigan scored in bunches were worth only five points in those days.

Michigan had fielded a normal football team in 1900, one that posted a 7-2-1 record and scored 117 points. Then Michigan hired Fielding H. (Hurry Up) Yost to coach the Wolverines, and the course of football history was changed. In his 1901 debut on the Ann Arbor campus, Yost's team ran up 50 points on a surprised

Albion College team. Four weeks later, they tallied 128 against Buffalo. In another game, they had 89.

Their amazing scoring machine was invited to visit Pasadena and play Stanford University in what would be the forerunner of post-season bowl games on New Year's Day, 1902. Michigan agreed to make the trip to the Tournament of Roses, but after training in snowy Ann Arbor the team found the hot West Coast weather much to its disadvantage.

Against Stanford, the Wolverines got off to a sluggish start. Both teams traded punts and field position back and forth for about 23 minutes. Then Willie Heston, a halfback and the greatest star of the Point-A-Minute era, broke loose with a run that set up a touchdown. Michigan grabbed a half-time lead of 17-0.

The second half was a walk-through as Michigan could not be stopped. Heston didn't score a TD, but he gained nearly 200 of Michigan's 504 yards. Teammate Neil Snow scored five times. When the score reached 49-0 with several minutes to play, Michigan had yet to substitute, and Stanford players were getting injured one after the other. The game was called by mutual agreement.

For the season, Michigan had swept past 11 opponents, scoring 550 points. It would be the Wolverines' *lowest* total until 1905, when they scored 495. No one scored on Michigan in 1901.

In 1902, Michigan outscored the opposition, 644-12 in 11 games. In 1903, it was 565-6, though a tie with Minnesota spoiled an otherwise unblemished record. In 1904, the Wolverines were unbeaten again, outscoring opponents 567-22 in 10 games.

That was Heston's last year. In four seasons, he had scored 72 five-point touchdowns, far more than anyone in college football history. He had never played in a losing game.

But the Wolverines, who had topped 100 points four times with Willie in the lineup, learned to live without him in 1905. For most of the season, they did nicely. In their first 12 games, the Wolverines were unbeaten and unscored-on, and scored 495 points. Then in the season finale, Michigan lost to Chicago, 2-0. It was the first defeat in 57 games.

In five years, Michigan gave up only six TDs, and only two of them came as the result of sustained drives.

During that time, Michigan topped 100 points four times, including a high of 130 versus West Virginia; it topped 80 points five other times. All in all, Michigan went over the coveted 60-point mark 20 times, including a 75-point splurge the week before it lost to Chicago.

Never again would college football see such scoring. But in their next trip to the Rose Bowl, in 1948, Michigan offered a reminder of days gone by. The Wolverines won, 49-0, again.

The Point-A-Minute Teams

1901

Mich.		Opp.
50	Albion	0
57	Case Tech	0
33	Indiana	0
29	Northwestern	0
128	Buffalo	0
22	Carlisle	0
21	Ohio State	0
22	Chicago	0
89	Beloit	0
50	Iowa	0
49	Stanford*	0

*Rose Bowl

1902

Mich.		Opp.
88	Albion	0
48	Case Tech	6
119	Michigan State	0
60	Indiana	0
23	Notre Dame	0
86	Ohio State	0
6	Wisconsin	0
107	Iowa	0
21	Chicago	0
63	Oberlin	0
23	Minnesota	6

Team Records

1903

Mich.		Opp.
31	Case Tech	0
79	Beloit	0
65	Ohio Northern	0
51	Indiana	0
88	Ferris Inst.	0
47	Drake	0
76	Albion	0
6	Minnesota	6
36	Ohio State	0
16	Wisconsin	0
42	Oberlin	0
28	Chicago	0

1904

Mich.		Opp.
33	Case	0
48	Ohio Northern	0
95	Kalamazoo	0
72	Chicago P. & S.	0
31	Ohio State	6
72	Amer. Medical	0
130	West Va.	0
28	Wisconsin	0
36	Drake	4
22	Chicago	12

1905

Mich.		Opp.
65	Ohio Wesleyan	0
44	Kalamazoo	0
36	Case Tech	0
23	Ohio Northern	0
18	Vanderbilt	0
31	Nebraska	0
70	Albion	0
48	Drake	0
33	Illinois	0

Incredible Football Feats

40	Ohio State	0
12	Wisconsin	0
75	Oberlin	0
0	Chicago	2

Notre Dame Had 53 Pro Football Candidates On Campus In One Season

There's no official record for the number of players from one school who go on to professional football, but it would be difficult to top the 1947 Notre Dame squad. That year at South Bend, the Irish had gathered at least 53 players, including freshmen who were ineligible for varsity ball, who went on to the pros. Considering the fact that there were fewer pro teams then than now, the figure is astonishing.

Just about anybody who was anybody on that great Notre Dame squad got a pro contract after he got out of school. Among the stars were three quarterbacks—All-America Johnny Lujack, backup man Frank Tripucka and freshman Bobby Williams. On the line, George Connor, the captain and star tackle, and Leon Hart, a future Heisman winner and end, would be top picks. So would All-Americas Emil Sitko, a fullback, and

Bill Fischer, a guard. Jim Martin, an all-around lineman, and Jerry Groom, a center, would be among the other future pro stars.

Just about the only player of note without a pro future was little halfback Terry Brennan, the team's leading game-breaker and scoring leader. He later came back to Notre Dame as head coach.

If the Irish of that vintage were prolific in providing future pros, it was no wonder. The 1947 Notre Dame team was considered the best ever in the school's sparkling history. They won all nine games, scoring 291 points to 52 for the opposition. Only Northwestern came close to the Irish at the final gun, and Notre Dame won that game by eight points. The Irish were in the midst of four straight unbeaten seasons.

* * *

There's no official record for most players taken in the regular annual football draft in a single season either. But the honor apparently belongs to the 1970 Ohio State team, which had 13 players taken in the NFL draft.

Four of the Buckeyes were picked on the first round, including John Brockington, who went on to become Rookie of the Year as a Green Bay Packer fullback.

* * *

For high draft choices, however, even Ohio State can be matched by a rival within its own Big Ten conference. After the 1966 season, in which Michigan State battled Notre Dame to a tie for the national title, four Spartans were chosen among the first eight players taken in the (1967) draft. Tackle Bubba Smith, linebacker George Webster, and end Gene Washington went 1-2-3. Running back Clint Jones was the eighth man chosen.

Chicago Bears Won An NFL Championship Game By An Astounding 73-0 Score

Quarterback Sammy Baugh of the Washington Redskins had played enough football in his lifetime to know a "whupping" when he saw one. After his team went down to defeat to the Chicago Bears in the 1940 National Football League championship game, Baugh was asked what would have happened if the Redskins had scored first. His answer was simple and direct: "We would have lost 73-7."

Never in pro football history had one team lambasted another so badly as the Bears did the Redskins in 1940. Though it was a day of infamy in the nation's capital, at least the Redskins took the defeat realistically.

The Skins had beaten the Bears, 7-3, three weeks earlier that season, so a tight playoff game was expected. The Washington team went into the December 8 contest with a 9-2-0 record and the Chicago eleven with 8-3-0, so the matchup couldn't have seemed closer. But pre-game prognostications were as close as the Redskins would get. This was a day for the Bears to rule, right from the start. As sports columnist Arthur Daley of the New York *Times* wrote, "This was the day the Humane Society took off."

The fact that the contest was held in Washington's Griffith Stadium on a beautiful afternoon added to the insult.

The Bears, brilliant in their explosive T-formation offense, zipped downfield to score 56 seconds after the opening kickoff, as fullback Bill Osmanski dashed 68 yards. Before the quarter was over, Chicago had a 21-0 lead. The Bears scored again in the second period and from then on the only contest was between the Chicago offense and the Chicago defense. Coach George Halas played all 33 of his men; 15 of them figured in the final scoring.

Some 36,000 Washington fans sat silently through the footraces to the goal line by Chicago players.

In the second half, the Chicago defense began grabbing its share of the glory as the Redskins began to play catch-up football. Touchdown No. 5 came after Baugh intended a pass for one of his receivers deep in his own territory. The Bears' Hampton Pool swiped it out of the air and ran it back for a TD. After the sixth Bear TD, the Bears' George McAfee stole a pass and carried it 34 yards to the end zone. Later, Bulldog Turner returned a 21-yard interception to score. The Bears scored again, and then again as Turner fell on a fumble on the 2-yard line to set up the Bears' tenth touchdown. By now, the Bears had surpassed the NFL scoring record with their 67th point.

After that, there was another interception which touched off a scoring drive. The Bears drove again and made the score 73-0.

Once during the game the Redskins drove to the Bear 6-inch line. Appropriately the drive stalled there.

It was hardly a game, much less a contest, but the Bears' George Halas, who fashioned 321 victories in his pro coaching career, said he felt it was a pivotal game in football history. For one thing, he analyzed, it touched off the era of the T-formation; "People who never used the T before put it in immediately," he said. "They didn't use anything else for the rest of their lives."

He added, "Since then, football hasn't been the same. The game made us a major league."

One only has to look at the rise in pro football attendence and attention from that day on to realize that Halas must have been right—despite the zany score.

Georgia Tech Once Scored A 222-0 Victory

The problems for Cumberland College began before the little school's football squad boarded the train for Atlanta to play powerful Georgia Tech on October 7, 1916. Cumberland was to be one of those early-season warmup games for Tech, which was just coming off an unbeaten campaign. But the Lebanon, Tennessee, team began miscalculating at about the same time it accepted a $500 guarantee to go to Atlanta. For one thing, there was a problem in rounding up enough healthy bodies to compete against the Yellowjackets; Cumberland's team was fairly informal. Cumberland also failed to acquire a handful of Vanderbilt regulars, despite a previous, somewhat unscrupulous agreement. Finally, when the Cumberland squad was assembled for the trip, three players missed the train.

Butch McQueen, the Cumberland law student

who served as the team's coach, ordered his club aboard, anyway, confident that he could match wits with Tech coach John Heisman.

At Atlanta's Grant Field, about 1,000 fans showed up, expecting to see a possible replay of the previous week's 61-0 victory over Mercer. Cumberland was that bad and Tech fans knew it.

Coach Heisman, for whom the famous football trophy is named, was a brilliant strategist. For a moment before the kickoff, however, his own fans may have disputed that fact. He ordered Tech to kick off, rather than receive, after it won the pre-game coin toss.

That decision alone gave Cumberland an opportunity to make its big rushing play of the game. After the regular quarterback was knocked unconscious on the first play, Morris Gouger stepped in at the position and plowed into the Tech line. His 3-yard gain would become one of Cumberland's brighter moments.

During the game, Cumberland would compile a minus-45 yards rushing, partly the result of nine fumbles. Two of 11 passes would go for 14 yards.

Meanwhile, Tech started off its day by returning Cumberland's first punt to the 20 and scoring on the very next play. Cumberland dropped the ensuing kickoff and it was scooped up by a Tech player and hauled in for a second TD.

When Cumberland fell behind, 28-0, McQueen changed his strategy and decided to kick off after the Tech TDs. But that didn't work either. Before long Tech led 42-0.

Cumberland tried receiving again but couldn't move the ball, and Tech scored once more. So Cumberland tried kicking off but Tech hauled it back 90 yards for yet another TD. The quarter ended with the Yellowjackets in the lead, 63-0. Tech exactly doubled that score by halftime.

Tech didn't show any real mercy in the second half, but it did start giving the ball to people like tackles. They scored, too. In fact, Tech began to score every time it got the ball.

Cumberland's lone "drive" came on a 10-yard pass. But the play got the Tennessee school nowhere. They were at third down and 28 when the big gainer took place.

Stories have been passed down through the years as to what happened in the final minutes of this historic game. Rumor has it that Cumberland players were seen huddling on the Tech bench, hoping that their own coach could not find them and make them go back into the game. Another legend relates that a fullback, fearful of being pounced on by Tech players, refused to heed a teammate's shout to fall on a fumble. His reply: "Not me. I didn't drop it."

Tech gained 528 yards rushing that day and another 440 yards on kick returns. But the final score—222-0—is the statistic that has stood up over the years. Never before or after has a college team topped the 200 mark.

Two years later Tech was at it again. In 1918, the Yellowjackets rolled up more than 100 points against three different opponents. Cumberland wasn't one of them. The little team had had enough of the big time in 1916.

The Most Prolific Scoring Prep Teams?

In 1919, Harrisburg (Pennsylvania) Tech put
it all together. In its 12 games that season, Tech
scored a total of 701 points, for a per-game average of 58.4.

Tech's opponents weren't so prolific. All together they scored a total of zero points.

*   *   *

For a single-game record, the slaughter that
Haven (Kansas) High administered to Sylvia
High in 1928 stands out. Haven won that contest
with no trouble, 256-0.

During the season, Haven High poured it on
a few other opponents, too. The combined scores
were Haven, 578 points; Opponents, 0.

*   *   *

Undefeated, untied and unscored-on high-school elevens are found not only in the dark ages of American football. In 1973, Arthur Hill High School of Saginaw, Michigan, outscored its nine foes, 443-0.

MISCELLANEOUS

Doak Walker Figured In Every NFL
Statistical Category In 1955

When Doak Walker left the campus of Southern Methodist University in 1950, the football world figured he had left his fabled career behind. At SMU, Walker had performed miracles week after week, passing, running and kicking the football. He was a three-time All-America and a Heisman Trophy winner. Many years later, *Life* magazine would characterize him as the "last of the genuine college football heroes" as far as campus adulation was concerned.

The pros were something else. First of all, Doak weighed little more than 170 pounds, and there were days when, after running, passing and kicking, he would come out of a game weighing only 155. The Detroit Lions, however, figured he was worth a first-round draft choice (they had two of them that year and made Doak their second) if not just as a drawing card alone.

Walker did not let the Lions down. In his first season, he led the National Football League in scoring and his point total—128—was the second highest on record at the time.

"The Doaker" was great to the end in the pros, even if he did retire somewhat prematurely after the 1955 campaign. He was all-pro halfback in four of his six seasons and led the Lions into the title game three times, two of which they won. He led the league in scoring in both his first and final seasons and he set a Lion career scoring record of 534 points.

But for all his feats in football, an obscure one in his final season may have been his most remarkable. In 1955, Doak Walker figured in all ten of the NFL's statistical categories. It was no fluke; Walker ran, passed, caught passes, placekicked, punted, ran back kicks and intercepted a pass as part of his week-by-week chores.

The fact that he was injured often during that final year made his statistics more amazing.

Here's Walker's record for 1955:

Rushing: Ran 23 times for 95 yards (including a 51-yard TD jaunt) and two touchdowns. Averaged 4.1 yards a carry.

Passing: Attempted three and, for the first year in his career, completed none.

Receiving: Caught 22 for 428 yards (including a 70-yarder) and five touchdowns. Averaged 19.5 yards a catch.

Extra Points: Made 27 of 29.

Field Goals: Made nine of 16 (including a 41-yarder).

Scoring: Had 96 points (tops in league).

Punting: Booted nine for a 40.2-yard average when Detroit's regular punter got hurt. Walker was never a regular punter in the pros.

Punt Returns: Had two for 5 yards.

Kickoff Returns: Had one for 24 yards.

Interception: Had one for 20 yards.

If Doak Walker's record for getting into the statistical columns endures, it will probably be because of pro football's specialized nature today. The O. J. Simpsons don't punt, and the Joe Namaths don't intercept passes, and the Garo Yepremians don't run back kicks. But then again the Doak Walkers don't come along with any regularity either.

Mrs. Pat Palinkas Played Pro Football

Like many minor-league professional sports franchises, the Orlando Panthers of the Atlantic Coast Football League were looking for a gimmick to spruce up the attendance for the 1970 season. The Florida team looked hard—but not far. The Panthers decided to utilize a woman player in their August 15 game with Bridgeport, Connecticut. Their candidate for the manly chore was 27-year-old housewife Pat Palinkas, whose husband just happened to be the Panther placekicker.

Pat had held the football on the kicking tee in the past while her husband practiced, so the Panthers were not exactly introducing the game to a neophyte. The team announced that she would enter the roster and would hold for her husband.

Funny, right?

Well, one of the Bridgeport players didn't think so.

As Pat lined up the ball after the Panthers' first touchdown, in swooped defensive lineman Wally Florence, who had been trying to eke out a living in football after starring at Purdue University seven years before.

When Pat fumbled the center's passback, the 235-pound Florence crushed her into the ground, soiling her brand-new No. 3 jersey. At 5' 6" and 122 pounds, Pat was at once both the smallest and sorriest player in pro football.

Pat held for two more kicks, which were good as the Panthers won, 26-7.

If she was sore, Florence wasn't sorry.

After the game, he told newsmen who had gathered for the historic event: "I tried to break her neck. I don't know what she's trying to prove. I'm out here trying to make a living and she's out here prancing around, making a folly out of a man's game."

End quote.

And nearly the end of Pat Palinkas' career. She retired shortly thereafter.

Reynolds Played The Full 60 Minutes In 3 Consecutive Rose Bowl Games

Modern football players may be durable, but the two-platoon system and emphasis on specialists don't allow them to be tested for their staying power under game conditions. But even if they were given the opportunity, it is doubtful that anyone would ever match the record established in the mid-1930s by Stanford University tackle Bob Reynolds.

On January 1, 1934, Reynolds played the full 60 minutes in the Rose Bowl against Columbia. It's difficult to pin down what the 6' 4", 220-pounder from Okmulgee, Oklahoma, did, but he must have been pinning down somebody on defense. The Stanford Indians held Columbia to 77 yards and just five first downs rushing. Unfortunately, Stanford lost, 7-0.

The next New Year's Day, Stanford again was in the Rose Bowl, this time against the famous

150

Alabama team that featured Don Hutson. Thanks to Reynolds going both ways again for the full 60 minutes, Stanford got the best of the Crimson Tide in the running game. But Hutson had a field day on passes. Stanford went down again, this time 29-13.

Out West, many fans were cheering for Stanford to make it to the Rose Bowl again in 1936. It would give the famed "Vow Boy" team a chance for revenge and the All-America left tackle an opportunity to set a record that might be matched but could never be beaten—that of playing three straight 60-minute Rose Bowl games.

The Indians had a banner season, limiting their opponents to only 13 points, and were the natural choice to represent the West Coast in the 1936 Rose Bowl. Led by Reynolds in that game against Southern Methodist's national champions, the Indians held the Mustangs to a mere 40 yards on the ground. Reynolds played his 60 minutes again as Stanford won, 7-0. Wrote Braven Dyer of the Los Angeles *Times,* "It is questionable if there is a better tackle in the country than Bob Reynolds was this day."

In later years, Reynolds' name would be linked to sports again. As owner of several West Coast radio stations, the former Stanford tackle started the California (née Los Angeles) Angels baseball franchise.

Phipps Quarterbacked Purdue University To 3 Straight Victories Over Notre Dame

People don't go around knocking off Notre Dame's football team year after year. Rarely has a Notre Dame team lost three straight years to the same team. And some of those defeats came after the Irish put up a pretty good struggle.

But then came Purdue University quarterback Mike Phipps, a baby-faced assassin. The Irish had fine teams during the years 1967, 1968, and 1969—but Phipps was finer.

In the first of those seasons, he guided the Boilermakers to a 28-21 triumph over the 8-2-0 Irish at Lafayette. The next year, in another high-scoring contest against a 7-2-1 Notre Dame team, Phipps guided Purdue to a 37-22 victory. In 1969, it was Phipps again on the long end of the score, this time 28-14 over an 8-2-1 Notre Dame team.

For years, the Boilermakers had been known

as the "Spoilermakers" for their knack of upsetting top-ranked teams. But with Phipps in the lineup during the 1960s, even Notre Dame had to admit they were beaten fair and square.

Capozzoli, At Age 14, Gave Prep Record Keepers Something To Write About

As an 11- and 12-year-old football prospect, Tony Capozzoli of East Norwich, New York, was already showing the promise that would later get him into the record books. Twice the young Long Islander won the national Pass, Punt & Kick championship that takes place in front of the Super Bowl crowd. As a sub-teenager, he could punt a ball 55 yards, place-kick it (for distance) 61 yards, and pass it 58. No wonder high schools near his home coveted the youth when he got ready to enroll as a freshman in 1972.

Tony chose St. Dominic's High School of Oyster Bay, New York. The choice was easy: his dad Tom was the coach there.

At 14, Tony had already grown to near-professional proportions. He was 5′ 10″ tall and weighed 190 pounds. His father wasn't playing favorites when he installed Tony into St. Dominic's starting lineup.

The youngster responded with 103 completions in 175 throws (a percentage of 59) for 1396 yards and 16 TDs. As a runner, he gained 455 yards on 63 carries and scored eight TDs. But his kicking game was even more impressive. Fourteen-year-old Tony Capozzoli punted for a 41.4-yard average, which was better than all but 10 of the 26 regular National Football League punters that season. In addition, he kicked three field goals, including one for 38 yards, and 27 of 29 extra points.

Seven Nesser Brothers Played For The Same Old-Time Pro Football Team

Nepotism hardly has a place on the football field, where men have to make it on their own. There have been brothers on major-college teams but usually two, not seven. Yet one of football's first professional teams featured seven brothers, as well as the son of one of the brothers.

The team was called the Columbus Panhandles, not because of their financial shortcomings but because the Ohio capital was served by the Panhandle Division of the Pennsylvania Railroad. Six of the Nesser brothers formed the nucleus of the team when it was founded to play professional football in 1906.

The Nessers were a railroad family based in Columbus. One of them, young Raymond, played only briefly. But Ted, John, Phil, Al, Frank and Fred—and later Ted's son—played for years in the early days of the professional game. One of them (Al) was still active in topflight competition in 1931, when he was 38. Phil played until he was 40 and Ted and Frank until they were 37. Fred Nesser played until he was 35. None of them could match John for staying power; he quit at age 46.

Though pro football may not have been the highly organized game it is today, the Nessers played in competition that was the best offered after the turn of the century. None of the brothers or Ted's son prepped for their part-time pro careers in college football.

For the Nessers, football was no easy task. They worked in the railroad shops as mechanics until 4 o'clock each day, grabbed their meals and took off for any point within 12 hours of Columbus to play weekend games. Then they would dash back to Columbus in time to be to work at 7 A.M. Monday morning. Their uniforms proudly bore the colors of the Pennsy Railroad—gold and maroon.

Father Nesser reportedly served as the team's manager while the mother washed and mended the uniforms. Only one male member of the Nesser clan did not play football as a pro. He was 350-pound Pete.

Hayes Proved Himself To Be Speed "King Of The Hill" Of Pro Football

There is no statistic bandied about more loosely in professional football (and colleges and high schools, too) than the unofficial statistic—a man's speed. Press books, sports pages, and the television airwaves are saturated with tales of men who have run the 40-yard dash in 4-point this and 4-point that. The figures are tossed around almost recklessly.

Unfortunately, the clockings are taken by football coaches who more often than not do not know the intricacies of timing athletes. Furthermore, since the clockings are taken individually or among team members, there is little way of comparing the best sprinters and coming up with the fastest man.

Bob Hayes had once proved he was the "World's Fastest Human" when he won the 100-meter dash at the 1964 Olympic Games. He also was the first person to run the 100-yard dash in 9.1 seconds. But those were triumphs of his past —the Olympic victory coming in 1964 at Tokyo and the record 100 taking place in 1963 at St. Louis, Missouri. When the 1972 football season began, Hayes had reached age 30 and was believed to be far removed from speedy clockings. In fact, Hayes, who has one of the highest yards-per-catch averages in football history, was having a struggle getting playing time with the Dallas Cowboys.

There were men who challenged his claim to "World's Fastest Football Human." Cliff Branch of the Oakland Raiders, Mel Gray of the St. Louis Cardinals, Earl McCullouch of the Detroit Lions and Richmond Flowers of the New York Giants were among the many "flyers" who had some track and field records in their own athletic careers.

The questions about Hayes lingered because he seemed to be on the downcurve of his career, ranking only fifth among receivers on his own team. His 13.3-yard-per-catch statistic was almost 7 yards off his lifetime average.

The off-season gave Hayes a chance to redeem himself though.

In an effort to attract fans from other sports, the new International Track Association added what it called a "King of the Hill" event to its pro track tour in early 1973. Hayes, who always maintained a love for the sport that first brought him national acclaim, was quick to sign up.

A man who lost only twice in the short sprints a decade before, Hayes showed the old zest on the tour after losing in his debut to Cliff Branch. Both men sped to 4.5-second clockings, but Branch beat Hayes by a nose.

After that there was no stopping "Bullet Bob." He began winning week after week until he collected first-place prizes in all 14 of the remaining sprints on the pro tour. When 9.2 sprinters like Branch and Gray pushed him, Hayes accelerated. In one of those situations, Hayes ran a 4.3 40—for a pro track record. The timers were legitimate, unlike the pro football coaches. And Bob Hayes again was the unquestioned "King of the Hill."

Yale's Student Manager Scored A Point In The Big Game Of The Year

College football's unsung heroes, contrary to popular belief, are not the anonymous guards who pave the way for touchdown runs but the student managers who do all the dirty work around the football field. Their only rewards are association with the football team and possibly a special manager's monogram.

In 1952, however, Yale University gave its student manager, 140-pound Charley Yeager, a special bonus.

It began as a lark, to loosen up a taut team during one of the Elis' better recent seasons. The team would throw passes to 5' 6" Charley in practice. After a while, Yale devised a fake extra-point play for him. The quarterback (the ball holder on the placement try) would get the snap from center, stand up and toss the ball to the eager Yeager. Yale even got a uniform—No. 99, the smallest one available—ready for him in case the game situation would dictate the prank play.

But as the Bulldogs rolled through the 1952 season, there was little hope that Charley would get into a game. As the season finale loomed ahead, against arch-rival Harvard, there seemed no chance at all. Yale and Harvard people call their contest "The Game" and treat it with gridiron reverence.

Still, Yeager got his name in the game program.

However, when the team packed its gear for the trip to Harvard Yeager had to do his chores as usual as student manager, heading the Yale staff in getting ready for the game.

When Yale rolled up a 27-7 lead by halftime, though, Charlie was told to get into uniform. This might be his day. After Yale scored a third-quarter touchdown, the manager got the word from the head coach, Jordan Olivar, to be ready to go in if the Bulldogs made yet another touchdown.

The Yale players, sensing the excitement that would enliven a game seemingly won, worked hard to get another score right away—and they did. Little Charlie Yeager dashed inconspicuously onto the field for the extra point. He lined up at right end.

But as the ball was snapped, Charlie got knocked over by a Harvard player. Yale's quarterback saw that, but his other receivers were having trouble, too, so he went right. Charlie bounced to his feet and continued into the end zone.

The quarterback threw and Charlie clutched the ball to his gut. He made his point for student managers all over the country.

Wilson Rushed For 98 Yards On One Play
—And Did Not Score

In 1946, a small-college back named Wilson, ripped off what almost was the dream run. He took the ball on his own 1-yard line for Ohio Northern in its game against a strong Otterbein team. He sprinted 98 yards before going down on the Otterbein 1.

*   *   *

Idaho University had a near-perfect performance, too, against its rival, the University of Oregon, in 1908. Idaho gained 347 yards and did not give up a single foot from scrimmage.

Oregon won the game, though, 27-21.